I'LL BE
SEEING YOU

"If it is possible, as far as it depends on you,
live at peace with everyone."

—Romans 12:18 (niv)

WHISTLE STOP Café MYSTERIES

Under the Apple Tree
As Time Goes By
We'll Meet Again
Till Then
I'll Be Seeing You

WHISTLE STOP Café MYSTERIES

I'll Be Seeing You

LESLIE GOULD

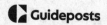

Guideposts

Whistle Stop Café Mysteries is a trademark of Guideposts.

Published by Guideposts Books & Inspirational Media
100 Reserve Road, Suite E200
Danbury, CT 06810
Guideposts.org

Cover and interior design by Müllerhaus
Cover illustration by Greg Copeland at Illustration Online LLC.
Typeset by Aptara, Inc.

ISBN 978-1-959634-61-4 (hardcover)
ISBN 978-1-959634-39-3 (epub)

Printed and bound in the United States of America
10 9 8 7 6 5 4 3 2 1

CHAPTER ONE

*A*lumni Night at the Dennison Depot was a resounding success. The buzz of voices, Glenn Miller's "Chattanooga Choo Choo," and exclamations of recognition filled the Whistle Stop Café along with the sugary scent of fresh doughnuts, apple cider, and pumpkin spice.

Owner Debbie Albright stepped out from behind the counter to clear orange paper plates and black napkins—the colors of the Claymont Mustangs—off the tables. She stepped to where Ray Zink and Eileen Palmer, the oldest of the alumni at ninety-eight and one hundred, respectively, sat. The evening had grown late for them, and they'd soon need to return to Good Shepherd, the retirement center and assisted-living facility where they both lived.

Eileen, her gray hair brushed back from her face and her blue eyes as bright as the overhead lights, wore her wool coat against the chill of the evening even though it was warm inside the café. Ray, his white hair neatly trimmed, wore his old Dennison High letterman's jacket from 1943, long before Dennison merged with another school to form Claymont High. He swayed a little in his wheelchair as Glen Miller sang about a party at the station.

"Don't you love this song?" Eileen asked as she snapped her fingers.

Ray nodded and grinned. Both he and Eileen appeared to be ready to get up and dance.

As Debbie picked up their empty plates and cups, Ray thanked her. "I want to go take a look at the model railroad. Could you wheel me through the crowd to the museum?"

"Yes, we'll need your steady hands." Eileen pushed her chair back.

"Certainly." Helping the elders of Dennison was one of Debbie's favorite things to do. "Let me put these in the trash." Once she was back behind the counter, she told her friend and co-owner of the café, Janet Shaw, she wouldn't be gone long. "I'm just going to escort Ray and Eileen to the museum."

Then she turned to Greg Connor, another friend, and said, "You should take a break when I get back."

"I'm doing fine." His stunning blue eyes twinkled. "But would you check on Julian? Tell him to come give Jaxon a break." Greg's mother, Paulette, worked in the café but had another obligation for the evening. Debbie was grateful Greg and his sons had offered to help. Well, Greg had offered their help, and the boys hadn't protested—at least not in front of Debbie.

"Go ahead and have some fun," Debbie said to Jaxon. "Things are winding down. The cleanup will be easy."

Jaxon untied his apron. "Thank you."

"Thank *you* for helping," Debbie said. "I really appreciate it." Not only did she appreciate the help, but she appreciated having a positive interaction with Jaxon. She and Greg were friends, and she wanted his sons to know they could trust her, but fourteen-year-old Jaxon had been standoffish so far. Hopefully that was changing. It had been a fun evening, starting with attending the varsity football game that Claymont won and ending with the alumni event.

Jaxon had already hung his apron on the hook and rushed out of the café before Debbie put the plates and napkins in the garbage. She laughed. "Guess he was in a hurry."

Greg lowered his voice. "His crush is here."

Debbie grinned. "Really?"

"Madison Palmer."

"Kim's great-niece?"

He nodded.

A couple of weeks ago, Debbie had attended one of Madison's volleyball games with Kim Smith, Eileen's daughter, who was the curator of the museum.

"Don't spy on him or anything." Greg winked. "But feel free to report back to me anything you see."

"Oh, I definitely won't be reporting a thing." Debbie grinned. She wasn't going to jeopardize any connection she might finally be forming with Jaxon, that was for sure.

After washing her hands, Debbie slowly pushed Ray's wheelchair as Eileen walked beside them through the wooden doors of the café and into the crowd of people in the main part of the depot. Over the sound system the World War II hit "I'll Be Seeing You" played. Ray hummed along, and Eileen practically danced as she walked. When the song ended, she said, "We really did have the best music."

"Yes, we did." Ray kicked out one foot from his wheelchair, making Debbie nervous he might trip someone—but she had to agree about the music. Even the sad songs seemed to bring hope.

"Kim said the model train is decorated for fall," Ray said.

"It is," Debbie said. "And it's adorable." They continued through the open area of the depot to the museum and then past the exhibits to the model train room. The 1920s layout, patterned after the height of the railroad days in Dennison, bustled with activity. Both a passenger train and a freight train chugged along the tracks. Crossing arms lowered and rose. Lights blinked. Tracks switched. Pumpkins decorated the outside of the model depot, and a black cat sat on a bale of hay, flanked by miniature stalks of corn. The volunteers had also added trees with changing leaves, which added to the seasonal feel.

Eileen let go of Debbie's arm and clapped her hands. "It's all so lovely! It reminds me of Dennison in autumn when I was a girl."

Debbie loved the stories from the past, especially about the Dennison Depot. Coming back to Dennison, opening the café with Janet, her lifelong best friend, and spending her days in the depot soothed her soul. There truly was no place like home.

Debbie never tired of watching the model train display, and obviously neither did Eileen and Ray. It gave her such a profound feeling of nostalgia, especially when she concentrated on the miniature depot, an exact replica of the building in which they currently stood. It gave her a sense of security. No, not everything could stay the same. But in Dennison, most everything that mattered did.

"I bought a painting of the depot at a yard sale years ago," Ray said. "At the time, I thought it would be fun to begin a collection of depot-related art pieces, but there weren't many out there." He paused a moment. "I'd like to show you the painting, Debbie."

"I could come by tomorrow afternoon." Debbie enjoyed visiting Ray and Eileen at Good Shepherd Retirement Center as much as possible. Her father had been the director for years, and she'd always felt comfortable there.

"Did you know that Bob Jennings made this model depot years before the layout was completed?" Eileen asked. "Marguerite painted it. Some of the other buildings came from their collection too."

Marguerite... Debbie tried to place the name.

"I didn't know Bob and Marguerite did that work," Ray said. "They used to live a couple of blocks away from me."

"In which house?" Debbie asked. She'd purchased Ray's bungalow five months before.

"Straight down the street," he answered. "The corner house on the east side."

Debbie could picture the house. A cottage that had probably been built around 1910.

"Marguerite lived there until she passed a little over a month ago." Eileen turned to look at Debbie. "Sofia—she's Marguerite's daughter—was hoping to keep the place, but an inspection showed it needs a new roof and repairs to the foundation. It will cost more than she has."

Sofia. Why couldn't Debbie place that name either?

"I didn't know that," Ray said. "I hope Sofia can keep the place if she wants to."

"Wait," Debbie said. "Marguerite and Sofia? The French war bride and her daughter?"

"Well, yes, Marguerite was a French war bride. And Sofia is her daughter..."

"That's how we—my friends and I—referred to them when we were younger," Debbie said. "We would see them walking downtown together. They were so well-dressed and coiffed and seemed so mysterious." She had thought it was such a romantic notion, to meet a man overseas during wartime, find lasting love, and then a enter a whole new life on a different continent.

Debbie had been enamored with the two women as a child. No doubt, the reason she took French in high school and college was because of her interest in them. Debbie even tried, when she was ten, to put her hair into a French twist because the mother wore her hair that way. For a while, she asked her friends to call her Deborah, instead of Debbie, because she thought it sounded French.

Ray spoke up. "Eileen, you and Marguerite were close, weren't you?"

Eileen's eyes grew misty. "Yes, we were, although it took a while for us to form a friendship." She pulled a tissue from her purse. "There aren't many of us left, Ray."

Before he could respond, someone raised her voice on the other side of the model train layout.

"Dad would let me ride to your house with Dylan." Madison, her blond hair piled on top of her head in a messy bun, spoke forcefully to Kim, whose dark eyes had grown large. "I ride with him all the time." The girl towered above her great-aunt. Behind her stood a young man wearing a black and orange Claymont High School sweatshirt. He was tall, dark haired, and appeared to be older than Madison.

"No." Kim spoke softly to her great-niece. "I'll give you a ride as soon as we're done here."

"Oh dear," Eileen whispered as she continued to dab at her eyes. "Madison has been having a hard time lately."

Madison appeared as if she wanted to say more, but then she exhaled and backed away from Kim. For a moment, Debbie thought the girl would head for the exit, but instead, she circled a quarter of the way around the layout to where Eileen was. "Hi, Grammy Eileen. How are you?" She bent down and gave her great-grandmother a kiss.

"Just fine." Eileen patted Madison's shoulder. "I've been thinking about you and praying for you."

"Thank you." Madison spoke sweetly, the opposite of how she'd spoken to Kim. "I'll see you on Monday."

"I look forward to it," Eileen said as Madison straightened.

Madison continued on halfway around the layout to where Jaxon and Julian stood. The other young man, presumably Dylan, followed her. Again, Madison's voice was sweet. "My dad has a model train set up in our basement. Of course, it's nothing like this. He doesn't even have a depot yet." She sighed. "I wish I could get him one. Too bad I—or someone else—can't get him this one. He'd love it."

Debbie winced at Madison's words. Hopefully none of the boys would take what she said seriously. It was a good thing the model train set was well secured.

Kim must have heard Madison, but she didn't respond.

Madison turned her attention back to all three boys. "Are they still serving doughnuts in the café?"

"Yes," Jaxon replied.

Madison smiled. "Let's go get some."

"I need to get going," Dylan said to her. "Will I see you before Monday?"

"Maybe," Madison said. "But Monday for sure."

Dylan waved and started toward the exit.

"Let's go," Madison said to Julian and Jaxon. She led the way, pulling her hair down and flipping it over her shoulder. The boys followed. It appeared maybe both of them had a crush on her, although Julian was only a seventh grader and Madison, along with Jaxon, was a freshman.

Debbie couldn't help but wonder how old Dylan was. At least a junior. Maybe even a senior.

Eileen clasped her hands together. "I didn't think Madison had any interest in her dad's model train. It would be nice if she'd work with Tony on it."

Debbie patted her shoulder. "Father-daughter projects are the best." But Debbie doubted Madison really had any interest in working with her father on his model train. All of her interest seemed to be in Dylan. Whoever he was.

A few minutes later, Kim approached the three and said, "Mother, are you ready to go back?"

Eileen shook her head. "Gayle's going to give us a ride."

"Oh? Gayle's in town?"

Ray nodded.

Gayle was Ray's little sister. She was a bit younger than the other two.

"She's still driving at her age?" Kim asked. "Isn't she over ninety?"

Ray nodded again. "Ninety-one."

"Even at night?" Kim sounded alarmed.

Ray chuckled. "Well, not back home in Columbus. Her daughter won't let her, but what Trudy doesn't know won't hurt her. At home

Gayle only drives during the day. Here in Dennison, because it's so small, she drives at night. A little. She's always been blessed with good eyesight." He pointed to the bench along the wall. "Eileen, why don't you sit while we wait for Gayle?" Ray's eyes sparkled. He definitely had a soft spot for Eileen.

"Kim," Eileen said, "I've been thinking more about Sofia's problem. The talk about the model depot made me remember something I hadn't thought about for years."

Debbie turned toward Eileen, curious.

"What's that?" asked Kim.

"Sometime in the early '60s, Marguerite went back to France because her mother was ill. She stayed for several months, nearly a year, until her mother passed. Sofia was in high school and stayed here. Before Marguerite left, she told me she'd hidden something in Bob's model depot that Sofia might need someday. Then she said, 'In case I don't come back, tell Sofia. She'll figure it out.'"

"Mother," Kim said, "what an odd story. Surely whatever she hid isn't still there. She donated the depot for the model display—she would have removed whatever it was before she did so."

"Well, give her a chance to look at the model depot," Eileen said. "See what she can find."

Kim sighed. "I'll give Sofia a call and see what she thinks."

Debbie felt as if she'd overheard more than she should have. "I need to get back to the café and start cleaning up."

Eileen reached for Debbie's hand and squeezed it. "Thank you, dear."

As Debbie turned to go, Eileen said, "Kim, what's going on with Madison?"

"She's upset with me," Kim answered. "And with her dad." She lowered her voice. "Dylan asked her to go to the homecoming dance tonight, and her dad wouldn't let her go—"

"Debbie! Debbie Albright?"

Debbie stopped abruptly. A man wearing a blue sports coat and gray pants stood in front of her. He was tall, had brown hair with gray streaks, and wore a docent badge.

"Carson Argyle? What are you doing in town?"

"Kristy and I returned last month."

"Kristy?"

"My wife. We've been living in Chicago," he explained. "But when my parents moved into a retirement community near Cleveland—my sister and her family live there—we decided to move back into our family home."

"Where did you meet your wife?"

He grinned. "Here. I married Kristy Dixon."

Kristy Dixon. That was a name Debbie hadn't heard in years. "I didn't know you two had gotten married."

"Yes. A few years after college."

"And you're back in Dennison now." Debbie wondered if she sounded as surprised as she felt. "And already volunteering here at the museum?"

"Yes." He sounded as enthusiastic as she felt about the structure. "It's literally a dream come true, something I've wanted to do since I was a child."

"And you haven't stopped in the café to say hello?" she joked.

"Oh, I did stop by after Kim told me you owned it. Didn't Janet tell you?"

Debbie put on a fake scowl. "No, as a matter of fact, she did not."

Carson laughed. "Well, I guess I know how I rate. I'll stop by again soon."

"Perfect."

Carson pointed to his left, to a small woman with dark, short hair at the far side of the room looking at the exhibit of Dennison's Golden Era. She wore brown slacks, stylish boots, and a twill coat. She had a large leather designer bag draped over her shoulder. "There's Kristy."

"Well," Debbie said, "I'll go say hi." She waved and quickly moved across the room, dreading saying hello to Kristy. She took a deep breath and smiled. "Kristy," she said. "Welcome back to Dennison."

"Debbie?" Kristy had a hesitant expression on her face. And no wonder. She hadn't been very kind to Debbie during their senior year. Nor their junior year.

"It's so good to see you." Debbie reached out to hug Kristy. There was no reason to hold on to a grudge—or appear to be holding on to a grudge at least.

Kristy practically fell into Debbie's arms and gave her a tight embrace. "It's so good to see you."

As they released each other, Debbie said, "I just saw Carson. I'm glad the two of you found your way back to Dennison."

"So are we." Kristy smiled. "Carson is a writer and can work anywhere. I'm a software developer, and my company allows me to work remotely. We're thrilled."

"Great," Debbie said. "I need to get back to the café."

Kristy took a step forward. "Do you have time for a quick question?"

"Sure." Debbie really didn't. She'd been gone far too long.

"Do you still go to Faith Community Church? I remember you went there during high school."

"Yes," Debbie said, chagrined at her ungracious thought. "Are you interested in going?"

"Yes."

"Sunday school is at nine thirty, and church starts at eleven."

"Thank you." Kristy put her hand to her chest. "I'll see you on Sunday."

"Great, see you then." As Debbie turned back toward the café, she frowned. People changed, right? Kristy must have changed.

After all, Carson married her.

As Debbie stepped back into the café, she was surprised to see a line at the counter and both Jaxon and Julian helping again, busing tables, with aprons around their waists and gloves on their hands. Madison sat at the table that had been vacated by Eileen and Ray, staring up at a World War II photo of the depot with a Salvation Army Canteen cart out front. The sleeves of Madison's jacket were pushed up, showing a gold bracelet on her right wrist with an *M* engraved on it. She touched it with her left index finger and then clasped her hand over her wrist. Perhaps Dylan had given her the bracelet.

Seated at the table behind her were Harry Franklin and his granddaughter Patricia. Harry had been a porter during World War II and then a train conductor for years after the war ended. Patricia worked as a private-practice attorney. They came into the café most mornings for breakfast—it was fun to see them in the evening. Debbie smiled at them, and they both smiled in return.

Janet motioned to Debbie. "Can you get another tray of doughnuts?"

"Yes ma'am." Debbie stepped behind the counter and to the sink. After she put on her apron, washed her hands, and slipped her hands into her gloves, she grabbed the tray of doughnuts from the kitchen and began placing them on plates. Ten minutes later, the rush ended, they closed the register, and Debbie high-fived both Greg and Janet. "Thank you for making all of this work." She turned to Jaxon and Julian, who now sat at the counter. She held up her hand to high-five Julian. He cooperated. When she took a step toward Jaxon with her hand up, he hesitated, but then he gave a lackluster effort. Behind him, Madison laughed and held up her phone. "Auntie Kim needs help in the museum. Jaxon and Julian, want to come with me?" She stood.

"Sure." Jaxon jumped down from his stool.

Julian looked at Greg.

"Go ahead. I think we're good in here." As Julian followed the other two out of the café, Greg gave Debbie another wink. She didn't say anything. She'd tell him about Dylan later.

A half hour later, Debbie told Harry and Patricia goodbye as they left the café. Within minutes after their departure, all the customers had cleared out, Greg had put the chairs on the tabletops, and then Debbie had swept while Janet bagged the cash from the register.

The boys returned to the café with two other boys.

"Hi, Brent and Monty," Greg said. "You're in town late."

"Dad's on his way back for us," the older boy said.

"He took their mom home," Jaxon explained. "Is it okay if Brent and Monty walk to our house with us? They'll text their dad to pick them up there."

"Sure." Greg turned to the older boy. "Tell your dad I'll be home in a few minutes."

"First, I need my football bag out of the truck," Jaxon said. "I want to get my stuff in the wash."

"So do I," Julian added.

"All right." Greg dug his key out of his pocket. "Bring the key right back."

"Has Kim locked up the museum?" Debbie asked Jaxon.

"Yes," he answered. "Everyone's gone. Kim took Madison with her."

"All right." They would just need to lock up the café and the front door to the depot. Janet ran the mop water as Debbie finished sweeping.

In no time, Jaxon returned the key, his gym bag draped over his shoulder, and then walked out of the café.

By the time Janet finished the mopping, Debbie and Greg had finished the other tasks. After they grabbed their coats and Janet and Debbie retrieved their purses, they all went out the door of the café into the depot. Greg's phone dinged, and he pulled it from his pocket. He froze.

"Everything all right?"

"It's Roger. He's out in the parking lot, where he was supposed to pick up his boys." Greg placed a call. A second later, he said, "Roger? Monty and Brent walked to our house with Jaxon and Julian. They said they'd let you know. I'm on my way there now."

There was a pause. "I'll call Jaxon. I'll tell him to tell Brent to give you a call."

Greg sighed as he placed another call. Thankfully, Jaxon answered right away. Greg explained what was going on.

Debbie could hear Jaxon say, "Sorry. Brent must have forgotten to text his dad. And he must have his ringer turned down. I'll tell him to call right now."

"Thanks." Greg ended the call and stuffed his phone into the pocket of his jacket.

"Everything okay?" Debbie asked.

"I think so."

Ahead, Janet had the exit door open, but as Debbie and Greg approached, Kim came walking through it.

"I realized I forgot the model depot for Sofia when I reached the house," she said to Debbie. "Sofia wanted to take a look at it tonight. Luckily, Barry is home, so I could drop Madison off and not worry about her sneaking out. Wait for just a minute, would you?"

Debbie knew Kim didn't like to be in the depot alone at night. "We won't move," Debbie said. As Kim hurried by, Debbie lowered her voice and said to Janet, "You should go ahead and get home. You have an early start in the morning."

Janet yawned. "It's definitely past my bedtime."

"It's not here!" Kim called out.

"Uh-oh," Janet said.

Debbie started toward the museum, and Greg and Janet followed her.

Kim stood in the doorway to the museum. "Where's the depot? I left it on the cabinet in the model train room."

"I haven't seen it," Debbie said. "Someone may have stacked something in front of it."

"Or stole it," Kim said. "I don't see it anywhere."

"Let's look," Debbie said. "Surely it's here somewhere. Maybe someone moved it."

Or maybe not.

CHAPTER TWO

*A*s Debbie searched the museum, looking behind exhibit cabinets and in and beneath cupboards, she overheard Kim on the phone. "I don't know what happened to it, Sofia. After I took it out of the display, I put it on top of the cupboard in the model train room. I took Madison home and then realized I'd forgotten it. When I came back, it was gone. We've looked all over and can't find it anywhere."

Kim paused. "I'll find it, I promise. But maybe not until tomorrow morning."

Kim paused again and then said, "I'll call first thing."

A moment later, she called out from the middle of the museum, "I need to get home. Obviously, the model depot isn't here."

They all gathered around. "Did anyone see or hear anything suspicious tonight?" Janet asked.

Debbie reluctantly said, "Madison said something about wishing she—or someone else—could get the depot for her father's model train set."

Kim sighed. "She was kidding."

Debbie said, "It could be relevant."

Kim shook her head. "It's not."

"You should check with her."

Greg ran his hand through his hair. "I'll talk to the boys too. I don't think they'd do anything like that, but sometimes kids can take something as a sort of dare when it wasn't meant that way."

"How about Dylan?" Debbie asked Kim. "What do you know about him?"

"Not much."

"Dylan Rhodes?" Greg asked.

"Yes," Kim answered.

Greg turned to Debbie. "He's the high school quarterback."

"Oh." Debbie had never seen him out of his football uniform before tonight, but she did recognize his full name now that Greg had said it.

"He's a good kid," Greg said.

"What grade is he in?" Debbie asked.

"He's a junior."

Dylan looked much older than Jaxon, but two years made a big difference when it came to teenagers.

Janet pulled out her phone. "I'll text Ian and see if he can stop by. He might have some ideas of where to look if someone did pull a prank. It happens pretty often."

"It's not like the model depot is worth much." Kim stifled a yawn. "Except to us. I can get one of the volunteers to make a new one."

"But your mom said this one dates back to the 1960s," Debbie said. "We don't want to replace it if we can help it."

"True," Kim said. "And just the fact that it's missing is quite a shock for Sofia. Her dad made the model depot, and her mom painted it."

"And then there's the question of what might be hidden in it," Debbie said. "Whatever that's all about."

"What?" Janet asked.

"Marguerite told my mom that she put something in the model depot that Sofia might need someday," Kim explained.

"How odd," Janet said.

"Well, the sooner we figure this out, the better," Greg said. "I'll call Jaxon."

Kim sighed as she opened her purse. "And I'll call Madison."

Janet took out her phone too. "I'll text Ian." Her husband was the chief of police.

Kim questioned Madison, her voice growing louder. "Yes, Madison, I was pretty sure you were joking."

Greg had a serious expression on his face as he said, "I just needed to check, Jaxon. We can talk more when I get home."

Both Kim and Greg ended their calls.

"Madison said she wasn't serious and that none of the guys would have thought she was," Kim said.

"Jaxon said he didn't take it," Greg added.

Janet looked up. "Ian's busy. He said he'll stop by in the morning."

"Hopefully the model depot will show up by then," Debbie said.

No one responded to that. Whoever took it must have had a bag big enough to conceal it. Like Madison's volleyball bag or Jaxon's or Julian's football bags.

Kim and Janet left, but Greg stayed as Debbie locked the main door to the depot. "Thank you for helping tonight and for waiting for me now." She slipped the key into her purse and zipped her sweatshirt.

"Of course. Where are you parked?"

"At my house." She took her gloves from her coat pockets. "I figured parking might be in short supply at the depot tonight, so I walked here after the game."

"I'll give you a ride home," he said.

She hesitated a moment but then said, "Thank you." It was chilly, and she was tired.

He was parked in the side lot. She climbed into his truck and fastened her seat belt.

"I'm pretty sure that neither one of my boys would take the depot," Greg said, "but I'll check their football bags when I get home."

"Good idea." Debbie winced. "Not that I think they took it either…" Did she sound as if she thought they did?

Greg smiled. "Have I ever told you how humbling being a parent is?"

Debbie chuckled. "Probably."

"Well, believe me. It is." He sighed. "And my boys are good kids."

"I agree," Debbie said. They were good kids, but they were also normal. "I remember what it was like to be in middle school and high school. They're complicated times."

"That's for sure," Greg said.

He pulled into her driveway. "I'll text you after I search their bags."

"Thanks." Debbie opened the door. "And thank you for the ride."

"You're welcome. See you soon."

Greg stayed in the driveway while Debbie walked to the house. Cornstalks and pumpkins decorated the left-hand side of both the steps and the porch. She unlocked her door, stepped inside, and waved. Then she locked the door behind her. She hung her sweatshirt and put her purse on the built-in entryway bench made from the same oak as the trim throughout the house. Then she stepped past the staircase and into the living room. The soft glow of the lamp she'd left on illuminated the cozy space. She loved her house. She especially loved that Ray and his sister had grown up in it and that Ray had lived in it until he sold it to Debbie six months ago.

Debbie had passed the house as a teenager on her way to school. She'd started out riding her bike, which definitely wasn't cool, but once she got her license, her mother let her borrow the family station wagon most days to drive.

Thinking about high school led her thoughts back to Kristy again.

She and Kristy had been friends all through middle school and until the beginning of their junior year of high school. But then Kristy changed. And Debbie's favorite earrings had disappeared. Debbie never had indisputable evidence, but she suspected Kristy. When Debbie complained to her mother, her mom had said Kristy's family was going through some things and perhaps Kristy was having a hard time. She didn't elaborate. Since it was a small town, Debbie often heard gossip about her friends' families, but she didn't hear anything about Kristy's. She'd suspected her mother was being overly sympathetic.

Debbie headed to the kitchen and flicked on the lights. The kitchen had been remodeled since she moved in, and it was just how Debbie wanted it. She filled a glass with water and took a drink.

If the depot wasn't found by the next morning, Debbie would tell Ian everything she could remember about the evening. Every person she saw. Every word she overheard. Sure, the volunteers could make a new model depot—but it wouldn't be the original one, not the one Marguerite Jennings had painted. And it would take a few weeks for the replacement to be completed. What was the model train layout without its depot?

Besides, what about the message that Marguerite had left for Sofia? Debbie hadn't told Janet that Sofia was the French war bride's daughter. She put her glass of water on the counter and headed to the living room, texting Janet as she did.

I KNOW, Janet texted back. MARGUERITE USED TO COME INTO THIRD STREET BAKERY. SHE LOVED MY MACARONS.

WHY DIDN'T YOU TELL ME?

IT NEVER CAME UP. SEE YOU IN THE MORNING. It was late for Janet—she needed to be at the café before the sun came up.

Debbie headed upstairs to get ready for bed. A half hour later, as she crawled under the covers, her phone dinged.

A text from Greg. I CHECKED THE BOYS' BAGS AND THE DEPOT ISN'T IN EITHER. BUT THEIR DIRTY UNIFORMS THEY CLAIMED TO WANT TO WASH STILL ARE. I ASKED THEM AGAIN. BOTH BOYS DENY TAKING THE DEPOT AND SAID THEY DON'T HAVE ANY IDEA WHO WOULD HAVE. I DON'T THINK THEY'RE BEING COMPLETELY HONEST THOUGH.

CHAPTER THREE

*S*aturday morning, Debbie arrived at the café at six thirty to the smell of freshly baked scones and pumpkin muffins.

She reached the kitchen as Janet was taking a tray from the oven. Janet wore dark-wash jeans, an orange T-shirt, and a black apron with a locomotive across the front.

"How are you?" Debbie asked.

"A little bleary-eyed," Janet said. "But other than that, my usual cheerful self." She grinned. "I've got the baking done and the food prepped."

"Great. I'll take the chairs down and get the register ready." As Debbie put her coat and purse away, she asked, "Did you tell Ian about last night?"

"Uh-huh. He said he'd stop by around eleven this morning and that when this sort of thing—an item that really has no monetary value—goes missing, it's usually a prank or has somehow been misplaced. Either way, it shows up pretty quickly."

"Good to hear." Debbie headed out to the dining area, took down the chairs, and prepped the register.

Then she flipped the sign to Open.

The next hour sped by with mostly coffee drinkers looking for a muffin or scone. By eight o'clock, people were ordering bacon and eggs. Thankfully, Paulette, Greg's mother, started her shift at nine, and Debbie floated between the kitchen and the floor. Paulette knew practically everyone in Dennison, volunteered at numerous charities in town, and was a no-nonsense but very caring woman. She also minded her own business, which was a comfort to Debbie as she got to know Greg better.

A little after ten o'clock, Kim came in for a cup of coffee to go. "Any luck finding the depot?" Debbie asked.

"No." Kim sat down at the counter. "I talked with Madison some more. She's adamant that she had nothing to do with the depot going missing. She even cried, which I haven't seen her do since she was a little girl."

Debbie wasn't sure if crying was a sign of innocence or guilt. "Janet said Ian will stop by around eleven. Who's watching the museum?"

"Sofia came in. She used to volunteer for me, after she retired from teaching."

"She taught here, in town?"

Kim nodded. "At the high school. French. She left teaching about thirty years ago to help care for her father."

"Oh." Debbie guessed Sofia was in her late seventies now.

"After her father passed, she volunteered at the museum until her mother needed more care," Kim said. "I hope she'll start volunteering again, once she gets Marguerite's estate settled."

"I hope she does too," Debbie said. "I'd love to get to know her."

Kim smiled, as if remembering something, and then said, "I called Carson Argyle to see if he could come in, but he has an appointment. He said otherwise he'd love to help."

"That's nice of him. Did you ask him if he saw anything last night?"

"I did," Kim said. "He said he saw a man in a black SUV hanging around in the parking lot, but that's all. That could have been anyone."

"Any other details about the man?"

"He couldn't see him clearly enough to get a description. He just thought it was odd that the man was out there a while and never came in."

"When did Carson leave?" Debbie asked.

"When I did," Kim answered. "He came out the front door with me."

"Did you meet Kristy?"

"Who?"

"His wife. She went to high school with Janet and me. So did Carson."

"I don't remember Kristy, and I didn't meet her last night."

"She was here. Petite. Short dark hair." Debbie wiped the counter as she spoke. "She had on a cute outfit—brown pants, tweed coat, designer boots and bag."

Kim shook her head. "I'll have to tell Carson to bring her around again and introduce her. I'd love to meet her." She stood and picked up her coffee. "Come down with Ian when he gets here. I'll have Madison stop by too. Do you think Greg and the boys would come?"

Debbie took her phone from the pocket of her apron. "I'll text him."

An hour later, everyone gathered in the main room of the museum while Sofia spoke with a group of visitors in the model train room. Debbie caught a glimpse of her through the doorway.

She wished she'd known her name all those years ago instead of always thinking of her as "the French war bride's daughter." Sofia had a thin frame and wore her silvery hair in a bun at the nape of her neck. She was dressed in a black pencil skirt, flats, and a sage-green poet's blouse.

Dressed in his uniform, Ian cleared his throat and said, "Hello, everyone, thank you for coming. Let's go through what happened last night. Kim, you start."

Kim explained that she left the model depot on top of the cabinet in the train room and had come back because Sofia wanted to examine it to see if she could find something her mother may have hidden. "I called Madison right away, because she mentioned to the boys"—she pointed toward Jaxon and Julian—"and Dylan Rhodes that she wished her father had the depot for his model train."

"I wasn't serious," Madison said. "No one thought I was."

"And we didn't take it," Julian quickly added. Jaxon stared straight ahead, his jaw set.

"What about Dylan?" Debbie asked. "Could he have taken it?"

Madison rolled her eyes. "No."

"Why would Dylan steal a model train depot?" Jaxon asked as if that was the most ridiculous idea in the world.

"Yeah," Julian said. "That would be crazy."

Ian wrote something in his notebook. "All right. What happened next?"

"At nine o'clock, after we closed the museum, I took the depot from the display and put it on the cabinet." Kim pointed toward the model railroad room. "But I forgot to take it with me. I left the museum with one of our docents, Carson Argyle. Madison and the boys had already left, and Madison was waiting in the car for me. I took her home and then planned to go over to Sofia's but realized I'd forgotten the model. When I came back to the museum, it was gone."

Ian made a few more notes. "All right. Do you know for sure that the depot was on the cabinet when you left?"

"Not for certain," Kim said. "But I think it was."

"Who was in the museum after you put the depot on the cabinet?"

Kim hesitated a moment and then said, "Madison and the boys. Carson Argyle, like I said. My mother and Ray for a few minutes after we closed. Ray's sister Gayle picked them up. They went out the back door. As you know, we only use it to take things in and out and for our elderly patrons. So they don't have to walk as far."

"Janet, Greg, and I were also here after that, of course," said Debbie.

"Do you usually enter and exit through the back door?"

"No," Kim said. "Not anymore, not since the debacle with the time capsule last month. All of us—staff and volunteers—enter and exit through the depot's main entrance now."

"Did anyone else use the back door last night besides Eileen and Ray? And Gayle?"

"No," Kim said. "But this morning Carson mentioned a man in the parking lot in a black SUV."

"Roger Dunn has a black SUV," Greg said. "He was waiting in the parking lot for his boys, Monty and Brent."

Ian jotted that down.

"I'm sure none of them had anything to do with the missing depot though," Greg added.

"Did Monty and Brent seem interested in it?" Ian asked.

Greg glanced at Jaxon.

"They weren't in the museum with us when Madison said what she did about the depot," Jaxon said. He shrugged. "No one mentioned it besides Madison."

Ian turned to the kids. "How about any of you? Did you use the back exit?"

All three shook their heads.

"Did you see anyone else use it?"

Julian shook his head so vigorously that Debbie was distracted enough not to hear what Madison and Jaxon said, but they both said something. Most likely *no*.

"All right," Ian said. "I'll check in with Ray and Gayle and Eileen." He jotted something in his notebook and then looked up. "And where can I find Carson Argyle?"

"He's living in his parents' house," Kim said.

"He and his wife Kristy moved back to town recently," Debbie added. "Kristy was at the event last night too."

"Okay." Ian closed his notebook. "How many other people were at the event?"

"Around a hundred," Debbie said. "All ages. I think Julian was probably the youngest. Eileen would have been the oldest. Do you want names?"

Ian shook his head. "I'll start with the people who were in the museum at the end of the evening." He turned to Kim. "Let me know if you hear anything. Or if someone returns the depot. Often in these cases, the missing item reappears as mysteriously as it disappeared. No one ever fesses up to taking it, but nonetheless, they return it."

Debbie had the distinct impression Ian had directed that last message to Madison, Jaxon, and Julian.

After the lunch rush, Janet headed home and Paulette took over the cooking. A while later, Kim and Sofia came into the café for a late lunch. When Debbie approached to take their order, Kim introduced her to Sofia.

"Can you sit down with us?" Kim asked after they ordered.

"I think so." Debbie glanced back toward the kitchen, where Paulette was filling orders. "Let me get your drinks and soup first."

The soup of the day was a harvest squash. It was one of Debbie's favorites. She poured a decaf coffee for Kim and a regular coffee for Sofia and then ladled up three cups of soup. She placed everything on a tray and carried it out.

A minute later, she sat down next to Kim and across from Sofia.

"I've seen you around, ever since I was a child," she said to Sofia. "It's nice to finally meet you in person."

Sofia smiled at her.

"Because of your interest in finding the depot, Sofia and I thought you should know more of the story," Kim said. "Well, as much of the story as we can figure out."

Sofia nodded. "I'll give you some background." She took a bite of her soup. "Delicious," she said and then began the story. "Mama moved to a boarding school in Paris in 1938 as a fifteen-year-old in hopes of getting into art school, which she did the following year, just before Germany invaded Poland. It was toward the end of her first year that Germany invaded Paris in May of 1940. She stayed in Paris through the war, even though her parents lived in Marseille. In late 1944, she met my dad. It was a whirlwind romance. They married, I was born, and then he returned to the US. She and I followed in April of 1947." Sofia paused a moment. "Adjusting to life in Dennison was difficult for Mama. She'd been used to living in a city and didn't understand small-town life. Her English wasn't as good as she thought. Some of the local women were suspicious of her. At first, only one befriended her." Sofia stopped and smiled at Kim.

"Let me guess," Debbie said. "Eileen?"

"That's right." Sofia ate another spoonful of soup and then continued. "Eileen was kind to Mama from the beginning. She helped her with her English. Encouraged her to pursue her art. Shared casserole recipes with her. Invited her to church. Our families were always close, and we were all so surprised and happy when Kim was born."

"Aw," Debbie said.

Sofia smiled at the memory, and then her face grew serious. "I really have no idea what Mama went through during the war. She wouldn't talk about it. But living in Paris under the occupation of the Nazis couldn't have been easy for a young woman. In all my memories of her, she was cool and collected, which came off as aloof to others. It was hard for her to fit in here, but Eileen stuck with her and was always loyal. Daddy told me once that he thought Mama would have packed up and taken me back to France if it wasn't for Eileen." She smiled at Kim again. "That's why it didn't surprise me when Kim called about Mama hiding something in the model depot and telling Eileen about it. It sounded like something Mama would have done. She had so many secrets. Secrets about her family, secrets about the war, secrets about where she squirreled away money and extra food. It took me a long time to realize it was because of trauma. Anyway, I'd ask her questions about the war, and she'd only give me half answers. I remember when she went back to France when I was in high school. I begged to go with her, but she said I'd be bored. In France? Never. But she wouldn't budge."

"So what do you think is—or was—in the model depot?" Debbie asked.

"I don't know. A key? A message? Last week, I found a letter that Mama wrote to me in 1961, when I was sixteen. That was when she left for France, and she must have hidden it for me to find in case she didn't come back. It said she had a collection of a hundred gold coins for me that were worth a significant amount of money. This is the first I've heard of them." Sofia lowered her voice. "If they are valuable, I could really use the money now. I retired early to take care of Daddy when he was ill. Now the house needs quite a few repairs if I'm going to continue living in it. Otherwise, I'll have to sell it. I'm hoping the coins are worth enough to help pay for the fixes." She shrugged. "Perhaps Mama cashed them in years ago, but I hope not."

"Do you think anyone else knew about the coins?" Kim asked.

"I doubt it. Mama was a very private person."

"Do you think someone might have taken the depot because they suspected something, perhaps a key, was in it?" Debbie asked.

Sofia shook her head, but Kim had a horrified expression on her face. "What if someone overheard what Mom said last night and decided to steal the depot?" She looked at Debbie. "Do you remember anyone else being close enough to hear?"

Debbie shrugged. "Just Ray." She thought for a second. "If there is a key in the depot, it could be to a safe-deposit box. Did your mother have one of those?"

"At one time, yes," Sofia said. "But I can't find a key or any paperwork. I've checked with the banks in town. It's a long process to determine if a deceased person even had a box, and a longer one to gain access if they did, if you don't have the key. But I'm thinking she didn't have it when she died. Important documents, an emerald ring, a pearl necklace, and her wedding set are all in a lockbox in her studio. I found the key for that."

Paulette called out that their order was up, and Debbie collected Kim's and Sofia's half sandwiches and brought them to the table.

"I can't stress enough how good the Palmer family was and still is to us," Sofia said. "Both Kim and Eileen were by my side for Mama's service."

"And your family was good to us too," Kim said. "Do you remember the king cakes your mother made for us every Christmas?"

Sofia nodded. "*Galette des rois.* They're really for Epiphany, but since not many people celebrate that here, she made it as a Christmas dessert."

"It was delicious." Kim licked her lips. "And the crepes and croissants. Your mother should have opened a bakery."

Sofia smiled. "She enjoyed baking, but her preference was painting."

"Tell me about her art." Debbie saw a family come into the café.

"It's hard to explain," Sofia said as Debbie stood. "Come by the house sometime, and I'll show you her paintings, the ones I have left."

"I'd like that." Debbie stepped away from the table, welcomed the family, and seated them, then handed each one a menu. Now there was even more of a reason to find the depot. If it led to them finding the missing coins, that could mean Sofia could stay in her childhood home. There was far more at stake now than just a vintage model.

The café closed at three, and by four Debbie had finished cleaning up and preparing for Monday. The day's specials would be chocolate chip scones, a brie and bacon omelet, and the pumpkin spice latte, which was her secret recipe. She wrote the items on the chalkboard, concentrating on her handwriting, and then added a pumpkin with a swirling stem.

Debbie loved autumn and always had—the crisp days, the changing foliage, and the decor of pumpkins, cornstalks, and scarecrows.

After she retrieved her coat and purse, she headed to the exit, locked the café door behind her, and then sought out Kim in the museum. She found her in the model train room, staring at the passenger train that was chugging past where the depot should have been.

When Kim didn't look up, Debbie asked, "Are you all right?"

Kim raised her head slowly. "Oh, hello. I didn't hear you come in." She smiled. "I'm fine. You done for the day?"

"Yes. I'm headed over to see Ray. He wanted to show me that painting he was talking about last night."

"I remember him saying something about a painting."

Debbie shifted the strap of her purse higher on her shoulder. "Wouldn't it be something if it was one of Marguerite Jennings's paintings?"

"Oh, I don't know how hers would have ended up at a yard sale."

Debbie knew all sorts of things ended up in yard sales, no matter how much they were valued at one time. But she didn't say so. "I'll take a picture and send it to you. Let me know what you think."

"All right. Have a good day off tomorrow."

"Thank you." Debbie was ready to have a day off. Owning and operating the café was a lot of fun but also a lot of work. "Bye."

"If you see Mom, give her a hug for me," Kim called out.

"I will!" Debbie pushed through the door back into the depot lobby.

Ten minutes later, she walked into Good Shepherd. A pot of yellow mums sat on the counter next to the sign-in sheet. The receptionist wasn't at the desk, so Debbie wrote down her name and the time. Then she filled out a name tag and stuck it to her shirt.

Behind the reception area was a stained-glass window of Jesus with a lamb in His arms. Sunlight streamed through it, making the red of His robe and the white of the lamb radiate color and warmth.

She took off in search of Ray, heading toward his apartment on the first floor. He sat in his chair in the sitting area outside his door, chatting with a woman Debbie didn't recognize.

"Debbie!" Ray rolled forward. "I'd like you to meet Gayle." He turned to his sister. "This is the young woman who bought our house."

Gayle, who had stylish short white hair, smiled up at Debbie, showing two darling dimples. "It's so nice to meet you."

"Likewise," Debbie said. "How long are you in town?"

"Until Wednesday." She chuckled. "My daughter would like me to stay longer, even though it's less than a two-hour drive and I can make it often if I want. It's good for my soul to be back in Dennison."

"What brings you here?" Ray asked Debbie.

"I was hoping to see that painting you mentioned last night."

He laughed. "Oh, that's right. I invited you."

Debbie grinned. Ray was sharp as could be, even if he did occasionally have a memory lapse. But so did Debbie. Everyone she knew did.

"You sit," he said. "I'll go get it."

Debbie sat next to Gayle, who said, "My daughter, Trudy, is okay with me driving in my town, but she doesn't like it when I go much farther. But I've never had a problem—no accidents. No tickets. Not even a parking ticket."

Debbie was impressed, but she could sympathize with Gayle's daughter. She didn't look forward to the day when her parents would need to stop driving, although that wouldn't be anytime soon. "Where are you staying?"

"We have a third cousin here. Once Ray decided to sell the old place, she offered me her spare bedroom when I'm in town."

Ray rolled toward them, a small canvas in his lap. When he reached them, he held it up.

"Goodness," Gayle said.

"It's so—surreal," Debbie said.

"Isn't it?" Ray handed the painting to her.

It was small, probably five by seven inches. It wasn't as illogical as some surrealist paintings—there definitely was a theme—but... "Do you have any idea who painted it?" Debbie asked.

"No." Ray put his hands in his lap. "Neither did the person who sold it to me at a yard sale, oh, twenty-five years ago or so."

The painting was of the depot, but it was so much more than that. A locomotive charged toward the station, spewing a column of smoke that rose to the dark blue sky and mixed with swirling clouds. A mirror had been painted into the smoke along with the outline of a woman. There was a shelf of books at the end of the depot, and an oversized key in the lock to the front door. Beside the door was a chest with the lid cracked open, showing gold coins. Depot, key, coins. Could that be a coincidence?

Debbie tried to hide her excitement. "Is Eileen around?"

"I believe she's resting," Gayle answered.

That was too bad. Eileen might know if this painting was Marguerite's style. "Do you mind if I take a photo of the painting?"

"Not at all," Ray answered.

Debbie put the artwork on the nearby table and shot an overview of it.

"What are you thinking?" Ray asked. "What do you plan to do with the photo?"

"Text it to Kim and ask her to show it to Sofia Jennings," Debbie answered. "Do you think it could be one of Marguerite's paintings?"

"No," Ray said. "She painted flowers. This wasn't her style at all." He turned to Gayle. "Do you remember Marguerite? She was the French woman who married Bob Jennings. They lived down the street."

"Of course, I remember them," Gayle said. "I used to babysit for Sofia. And I disagree with you. Marguerite painted more than flowers." Gayle gestured toward the table. "I never saw this painting before, but one time I saw a painting of a city—I think it was probably Paris. There was nothing flowery about it. It was dark and gritty. I think it was Bob who encouraged her to paint flowers. Maybe he thought they'd be more accepted by others in town, more relatable."

Debbie texted the picture to Kim as the siblings began talking about other people who lived on the block in the old days.

Kim texted back immediately. I'M IN THE MIDDLE OF SOMETHING BUT WILL LOOK AT IT WHEN I GET A CHANCE.

Debbie responded with a thumbs-up emoji and then slipped her phone into her pocket. She'd guess pretty strongly that Marguerite was the artist. If she wasn't, someone else in town knew about the gold coins too.

CHAPTER FOUR

*S*unday morning, Debbie stepped into the foyer of the church five minutes after Sunday school had already started. She stopped at the coffeepot on the hospitality table and poured herself a cup, and then she made her way toward the fellowship hall, where her class met.

She stopped at the door and peered through the glass. Pastor Nick, who often taught the adult class, was leading the group in prayer. After he said, "Amen" she pushed through the door and took a seat at the nearest round table.

"We have visitors today," Pastor Nick said. "I had the privilege of meeting them before class, and I'm guessing they won't be new to many of you. I asked them if they would introduce themselves this morning, and they graciously said yes. Carson, Kristy, would you come up here, please?"

Carson and Kristy both stood. He wore a black suit with a royal-blue tie, and Kristy wore a black skirt with a powder-blue sweater. They were an attractive couple, that was for sure.

They stepped to the podium as Pastor Nick stepped aside.

Carson cleared his throat. "Well, as Pastor Nick said, we're Carson and Kristy Argyle. We moved from Chicago into my parents' house here a couple of weeks ago. I grew up in Dennison, and

Kristy lived here during middle school and high school." He put his arm around her. "We're thrilled to be back, and we look forward to getting involved in the community and in this church." He looked at Kristy. "Did I forget anything?"

Kristy shook her head. "We really are happy to be back. Carson is working on a project about the US railroad system during World War II, so this is the perfect place for us to relocate." She glanced at Pastor Nick. "Thank you."

"Thank *you*," he responded as they started toward their table.

When Kristy saw Debbie, she grinned and held up her hand.

Debbie waved back just as Janet sat down beside her, beaming. "It's great that Carson and Kristy are here," she said.

Debbie nodded. "Is Ian coming?"

"No, he's seeing to some things," Janet said. "It's been a busy weekend."

Pastor Nick read the scripture, Romans 12:2. "'Do not conform to the pattern of this world, but be transformed by the renewing of your mind. Then you will be able to test and approve what God's will is—his good, pleasing and perfect will.'" Then he said, "This is a great verse for New Year's resolutions—and here it is only October. But I wanted us to discuss ways we can make real changes."

A couple of times, Carson offered his thoughts on renewing one's mind, including making time to be still and listen to the Lord. Kristy stayed silent.

Janet said that she thought different stages in life called for different methods of renewing one's mind. With their daughter off to college, both she and Ian had entered a new stage. It was nice they had each other to help navigate the changes and challenges.

Debbie thought of the stages of her own life. Not many things in life stayed the same. There certainly were different seasons for different things and different ways of communicating with God. She thought of her human development class during her first year of college—it had been one of her favorite classes. She pondered how the stages of human development fit with the stages of spiritual growth.

After class ended, Kristy headed straight for Janet and Debbie's table. Janet stood and gave Kristy a big hug. When Kristy and Janet released each other, Kristy stepped to Debbie's side and gave her a hug too.

"It's so nice to be in the same town as you two again," she said. "I can't tell you how much it means to me."

Janet reached for Kristy's hand. "It's so nice to have you back. You kind of disappeared."

Kristy nodded. "My parents moved to Columbus a week after we graduated, and then I went to Ohio State that fall. I didn't really have a chance to come back to Dennison until Carson and I started dating our senior year of college. Then we just came to Dennison for short trips to see his parents."

Janet smiled at Kristy. "But now you're back for good."

"Yes, it seems that way." She hitched her purse higher on her shoulder. "We want to get involved and really make it home again."

"Well," Debbie said, "there are lots of ways to get involved. Lots of volunteer opportunities."

"It sounds as if Carson's already found a place at the museum," Janet said. "What interests you?"

"I'd like to do something with young people," Kristy said. "High school girls in particular."

Debbie was afraid she couldn't hide her surprise. "Oh?"

"Yes. Something that has to do with technology or design. Something that encourages girls to pursue studies and then careers in math and science."

"That's great." Debbie meant it. She had vague memories of Kristy excelling in algebra and going on to take calculus.

Someone waved from the doorway. *Greg.*

"I've got to go," Debbie said. "See you in the service."

As she hurried toward the door, Debbie overheard Kristy ask Janet, "Who's that?"

"Oh, some guy Debbie knows." Janet laughed. "Greg Connor. He was a few years ahead of us in school, enough that we didn't know him. We've all become good friends. *Just* friends." But Debbie could hear the wink in Janet's voice. She couldn't help but smile.

"Want to sit with me during church?" Greg asked as she drew near.

"Yes, please," she said. "Your pew or mine?"

They ended up sitting in "Debbie's pew," which meant the one her parents sat in and had for her entire life. Jaxon and Julian sat with friends, including Madison, a few rows ahead. Kristy and Carson sat between the young people and Debbie and Greg.

After the "transformation of the mind" Sunday school discussion, Debbie hoped the sermon might be on the eighth commandment, "Thou shall not steal." But the sermon was on Ephesians 2 "For it is by grace you have been saved, through faith—a not from yourselves, it is the gift of God—not by works, so that no one can boast."

The entire service was centered around grace, starting with the opening prayer and ending with "Amazing Grace."

Debbie felt convicted. Yes, whoever took the model depot needed to be held accountable, but Debbie also needed to be humble and full of grace in her pursuit of the truth. "Got it, God," she said.

"What?" Greg asked.

"Oh, did I say that out loud?"

He nodded.

She winced. Hopefully he didn't think she was losing it. Thinking out loud was a habit she'd gotten into from living alone.

After the church service ended, Debbie's mom spotted Kristy and headed straight for her.

"Mrs. Albright." Kristy leaned in for a hug. "How nice to see you."

Mom hugged her. "Oh, my. It's so nice to have you back in town."

As the two chatted, Carson approached Debbie and Greg. Debbie introduced the two men, and they shook hands.

"Has the model train depot been found?" Carson asked.

"No," she answered.

His face fell. "I assumed it would have been by now. Kim called me yesterday morning to see if I could help her out in the museum. She told me the model had gone missing Friday, but she said she thought it would turn up soon, that it had somehow been misplaced."

Debbie shook her head. "Any ideas what might have happened to it?"

"No. It was still on the cabinet when I left with Kim."

Gayle waved at Debbie from a couple of rows behind and then beckoned to her. Debbie excused herself and made her way toward Gayle, Ray, and Eileen. When she reached them, Gayle said, "I have a big favor to ask you."

"Go ahead," Debbie said.

"Would you be willing to let me look at the old place?"

"Of course," Debbie said. "I'd love that. When would work for you?"

"I'm leaving Wednesday."

"Then let's do it Tuesday evening. Come for dinner. Bring Ray."

Gayle clasped her hands together. "We'd be delighted." She turned to her brother. "Wouldn't we, Ray?"

Ray leaned forward in his chair, which was parked at the end of the row beside Eileen. "Wouldn't we what?"

"Love to have dinner at Debbie's, at the old place, on Tuesday."

"Of course we would," Ray said. "I always love going to Debbie's house." He gave her a wink.

Debbie smiled at Eileen. "You come too. We'll have a great time."

Eileen lit up like a Christmas tree. "I'd like that. Thank you, dear."

Greg waved at Debbie as he followed his boys up the side aisle.

Mom was still talking with Kristy, and now Dad was talking with Carson. Debbie admired both of her parents and remembered what Mom had said about Kristy's family all those years ago. Why had Kristy's parents left Dennison right after she graduated? Kristy hadn't said anything about where they were now, and Debbie hadn't asked.

She remembered going to Kristy's house a few times in middle school and early high school. Kristy was an only child—or maybe her siblings were all older and didn't live in Dennison.

Kristy's parents seemed older than Mom and Dad. Her father was a banker in New Philly. Debbie didn't think Kristy's mother had worked outside the home. She wished she could remember more.

As she watched her mother laugh about something with Kristy, Debbie noted how full of grace her mother was. It wasn't something that had come with age. Mom had always been like that.

Debbie would see her parents at Sunday dinner in a few minutes, so she didn't need to stay and speak with them now. She told Gayle, Ray, and Eileen goodbye and then went outside.

Janet and Ian were on the sidewalk under the canopy of fiery red maple leaves talking with Greg. Beyond them were Jaxon, Julian, Madison, and a couple of teenagers Debbie didn't recognize. When Jaxon saw Debbie, he turned away.

Ouch. Did he blame her for Ian questioning the three of them about the missing model train depot? Debbie didn't like how this was going.

Madison turned away from her too, but Julian waved with a grin on his face. At least one of Greg's boys liked her.

A half hour later, Debbie arrived at her parents' house on their double lot on the edge of town. Her mouth watered at the thought of Mom's pot roast, a dish she made at least one Sunday a month. Her other specialties were enchiladas, roasted chicken, and spareribs.

Debbie didn't realize until she was grown that cooking wasn't as easy as Mom made it look.

As she pulled into their driveway, she was surprised to see another car parked behind her dad's pickup. They hadn't said anything about having company.

There were three people in the yard looking at Mom's garden. Dad, Carson, and Kristy.

Mom had invited the Argyles for Sunday dinner. Well, maybe both Mom and Dad had invited them—but most likely it had been Mom's idea. There were other times when Mom invited someone without telling Debbie, and Debbie hadn't minded.

So why did it bother her now?

She opened her car door and climbed out.

Kristy started toward Debbie. "I hope you don't mind us crashing your Sunday dinner with your parents."

"Not at all." Debbie hoped her smile appeared genuine. If only she were as nice as Janet. "I'm happy to share Mom's good cooking."

Kristy beamed. "I haven't been to a Sunday dinner in—" She stopped. "I think at my grandmother's house back in Indianapolis during grade school was the only time my family ever did Sunday dinner."

Dad waved Debbie over to the garden. "I was just showing off Mom's pumpkins."

Most everything else had already been harvested and canned or frozen. Tomatoes, green beans, corn, peas, spinach, and squash.

Mom and Dad never said anything, but Debbie wished they could have been grandparents. The death of her fiancé, Reed, had been Debbie's greatest loss, but it had also been a loss to her parents.

They had loved Reed. And they'd hoped for a long and happy marriage for Debbie and most likely for grandchildren someday too.

They'd never said a word about her finding love again. They'd only offered words of comfort to her. One time Mom had said, "Reed would want you to go on with your life."

Mom was right. He would.

Neither of her parents had goaded her about Greg. They smiled when Debbie sat with him at church and other events. Both liked Greg. They'd known him long before Debbie ever met him. And they liked Jaxon and Julian too. Mom had taught both boys in Sunday school when they were preschoolers.

Her parents had always been against prying into her life, although they were always there for her when it mattered most, like when Reed had been killed in Afghanistan. They both took off work and came to stay with her, seeing to every detail of her care. Making sure she ate. Encouraging her to contact her doctor when she couldn't sleep. Communicating with Reed's family during the times it felt overwhelming to her to shoulder their grief too.

"Debbie?" Dad reached for her hand.

"What?"

"I was just asking if you remembered when we moved here."

She shook her head. "My first memory is here." She pointed to the mulberry tree. "Of you pushing me in the swing in the tree." She half expected the swing to still be there, but of course it wasn't. "I think I must have been three."

"I think so too," Dad said.

"Carson's parents lived in the same house all through his childhood too," Kristy said. "I've always been jealous of that. I lived in ten different houses growing up. The six years we lived here was the longest anywhere."

"I'm sure, like me," Carson said, "Debbie doesn't take her childhood for granted."

"No." Debbie squeezed Dad's hand. "I don't."

Later, over dessert—fresh apple cobbler—Kristy asked how long Mom and Dad had been attending the community church.

"I've been going to it my entire life," Mom said.

"And I started as a young man," Dad added. "I moved here at twenty-two for my first job, at Good Shepherd. And I stayed on until I retired."

"I was working at the clinic full-time," Mom said. "Later, after Debbie started school, I went back there part-time."

Dad speared an apple with his fork. "Becca did more than work, run our house, and care for Debbie. She volunteered at school and the church and helped me out with events at the retirement center. Becca makes so many lives in this town better."

It was true. Mom did. But mostly she'd made Debbie's childhood as wonderful as it could possibly be. And she knew her mom, and her dad, wanted her life now to be all it could be too.

CHAPTER FIVE

hat did Sofia say about the painting?" Debbie asked Kim when she came into the café Monday morning.

Kim froze.

"Remember the photo of the painting that Ray has in his room, the one he mentioned Friday?"

Kim gasped. "I forgot all about it." She took out her phone and began scrolling through her texts. "Oops. It was right in the middle of texts from Tony, and I lost track of it." She tilted her phone to get better light and then studied the image. "This is interesting, but none of Marguerite's other paintings looked like this. I don't think it's hers, but I'll forward it to Sofia now and see what she says." She sighed and rolled her eyes. "I forgot Sofia's flip phone broke. She's using her land-line now until she can get a new cell. I'll call and see if she's available."

Kim placed the call. It seemed to ring several times. Finally, Kim said, "It's Kim. Do you have a few minutes? I wanted to show you a picture of a painting. I don't think it's your mother's, but I could be wrong."

Kim listened and then said, "Is it all right if Debbie comes with me?"

After another pause Kim said, "We'll see you soon." She ended the call and turned to Debbie. "Can you sneak out for a few minutes? It won't take long. Sofia wants to see the picture of Ray's painting and for us to see the collection of her mother's paintings that she still has."

"I think that'll work. I'll check with Paulette."

Paulette, who was busing the table behind them, said, "No problem. Take your time."

"Thanks," Debbie said.

As she dashed into the kitchen to wash her hands and grab her purse, she told Janet she'd be right back.

"See you when you get here!" Janet grinned and returned to making a Brie and bacon omelet.

"I'll drive," Kim said as they headed out of the depot. Sofia's house was only a couple of blocks away, but Debbie needed to get back as soon as possible.

Debbie climbed into the passenger seat of Kim's car and buckled up. Kim sighed as she pulled out of her parking place.

"What's wrong?" Debbie asked.

"Madison." Kim put the vehicle in drive. "Tony isn't getting home until tomorrow." Tony was Kim's nephew. He and Madison's mom had broken up the year before, and Madison had chosen to stay in Dennison with her father instead of moving to Akron with her mother.

Kim exhaled. "I didn't think having a fourteen-year-old staying with me for a few days would be so hard. Thank goodness she has volleyball practice after school and I won't have to worry about her until dinnertime."

"Teenagers aren't easy, that's for sure," Debbie said.

"She's never been a problem before, but lately she's been unpredictable. And defiant, at times. But then she's fine out in public. Except Friday night."

"She seemed okay Sunday at church."

"She said she had a good time. Maybe because I was helping in the nursery."

Debbie had figured Kim volunteered somewhere on Sunday. She hadn't thought she would send Madison by herself to the service.

"Maybe it's me," Kim added.

Debbie shook her head. "I don't think so. I read one time that teenagers act the way they do so their parents—and relatives—will be happy when they finally grow up."

Kim smiled. "Or because their brains aren't developed and they're driven by hormones and emotions."

"True," Debbie said. She needed to remember that about Jaxon and Julian. Jaxon, especially, didn't come across as emotional, but that didn't mean hormones weren't wreaking havoc with his feelings.

They drove past Debbie's house. "Madison usually stays at my brother Neal's house when Tony is away," Kim said, "but he and Heather are at the same business event as Tony."

"I'm sure they're all really appreciative of your help," Debbie said.

"Oh, they are. I know that. I just feel as if this time has put a strain on my relationship with Madison, which I regret. I want to stay close to her."

Debbie understood.

Kim put on her blinker and pulled up in front of Sofia's cottage. "We lived just around the corner when I was a kid," Kim said. "In the Tudor-style house."

Debbie knew the house. It was one of the largest in the neighborhood.

"It sounded as if Marguerite's family had a large estate in southern France," Kim said. "She could have gone there during the war, where she would have been safer, but she chose to stay in Paris."

"She must have been a brave young woman."

"Oh, she was. Definitely."

Debbie followed Kim up to the front door. The house was painted light green with white trim. Both needed to be repainted. The porch spanned the length of the house and had trellises at both ends.

Sofia, wearing a black skirt, a gray sweater, and reading glasses on a chain around her neck, opened the door before Kim had a chance to knock. "*Bienvenue.*"

"*Merci,*" Debbie said as Kim said, "Thank you."

"Aw, *parlez-vous Français*?" Sofia asked Debbie.

"*Non.*" Debbie smiled. "I took it in high school and a year in college, but I don't remember much."

"That's too bad." Sofia led the way through the living room. "Mama's studio is in the back of the house." They headed through the dining room and the kitchen. Sofia pointed to the left. "This was a sunroom, but Daddy finished it for Mama's studio." She led the way through French doors into the room. The south side of the room was a wall of windows. Sofia pointed toward the interior wall. It was covered with paintings. All flowers. Daisies. Irises. Tulips. Delphinium. Cherry blossoms. They were nothing like the painting Ray had.

"Your mother's work is beautiful," Debbie said. She took out her phone and swiped to the photo of Ray's picture. "Did your mother do anything more surrealistic?" She turned the screen to Sofia. "Anything like this?"

Sofia took Debbie's phone and put her glasses on her nose. "I believe she could have painted something like this. She studied this sort of painting before the war broke out. But I never saw her do anything similar." Sofia handed Debbie the phone. "Is there a signature on the painting?"

Debbie shook her head.

"But it is of the depot, I could make that out."

Debbie nodded. "And a bookcase, a key, a mirror, a woman, and a chest of gold coins."

"Fascinating," Sofia said. "I'm definitely interested in seeing the chest of gold coins up close. Could I see the painting in person?"

"I'm sure Ray would be willing to show you. I'll give him a call." Debbie placed the call to Ray. After she explained what she needed, she put him on speaker. He suggested that Debbie and Sofia come to his place Tuesday afternoon.

"I can do that," Sofia said.

"That will work for me too," Debbie said. After they all decided on early afternoon, Debbie ended the call.

"Merci." Sofia smiled. "I am looking forward to the visit."

Back at the café, Debbie sat down in the office to plan for the Fall Foliage Train Rides that would take place the next two Saturdays. Whistle Stop would provide the cider and doughnuts at the depot in the canteen outside, as long as the weather held. They would also provide pumpkin sugar cookies as a treat on the train rides. Debbie needed to buy the ingredients for the doughnuts and cookies and purchase the apple cider from the orchard outside of town. Friday, they would prep for the event, and then early Saturday morning, Paulette would help Janet make the doughnuts.

Debbie sat at the corner table and made a shopping list, including paper cups, plates, napkins, and decorations for the canteen and the serving area on the train. As she finished her list, she heard Janet laughing.

Ian sat at the counter while Janet poured him a cup of coffee.

"Hi, Ian." Debbie stood and started toward them.

"Hello, Debbie." He pointed to Janet. "Just stopped by to see my lass."

Debbie grinned. "Good for you. How's police business today?"

"Slow, thankfully." He took the cup of coffee from Janet. "Thank you, love. I'm here to talk with Kim about the missing depot again and to see if she has any other ideas. I'd like to find it for her, if possible."

"So would I," Debbie said. "She didn't have any more leads this morning, but Ray has a painting that might prove helpful."

Ian cocked his head. "A what?"

As Debbie explained about Marguerite, the information from Eileen, and a possible key or clue of some kind and missing gold coins, she realized how ludicrous it all sounded.

Ian chuckled. "All righty then. Anything else?"

Debbie wished she had a towel over her shoulder that she could snap at him. Instead, she took out her phone and showed him the picture.

He squinted as he looked at it and then said, "Well, good luck with tying it into the missing model depot." He chuckled again. "I can't wait to see how it all works out."

Debbie laughed. "Neither can I. Mind if I go with you to talk with Kim?"

"No." He finished his coffee. "Come along."

He stood and blew Janet a kiss. "See you soon, love."

Janet waved. "I'm making shepherd's pie for dinner."

With a grin, Ian said, "I'll try not to be late."

When Debbie and Ian reached the museum, Kim greeted them. "I don't have anything to report about the missing depot."

"Except for a painting full of clues." Ian winked at Debbie, clearly enjoying teasing her.

Kim smiled. "Well, we don't have any evidence that the painting is Marguerite's or that it's connected to the model depot. But perhaps it will turn out to be."

Ian pulled his flashlight from his belt. "I thought I'd take another look around, just to make sure I haven't missed any clues."

"What can we do to help?" Kim asked.

"Stay out of the way." Ian winked again. "Kidding. Look for anything that's out of place, anything that's been moved."

"All right." Kim led the way into the train room. Debbie let the other two go first and stopped in the doorway.

She didn't notice anything out of order, and she imagined that if Kim had seen anything misplaced, she would have put it back. But who knew? Maybe Ian would come across something they'd missed on Friday and Saturday.

Ian ran the beam of his flashlight along the flooring and under the edge of the model train layout. Kim stepped to the far end of the room, past the cabinet where she'd placed the model depot on Friday night. Ian continued his thorough inspection, moving away from the display case. He ran the light beam along the base of the cabinet as Kim stepped farther away.

Then he shone it between the cabinet and the wall. "There's something shiny back there." He knelt and reached behind the cabinet.

Then he stood, holding up a bracelet. "Do either of you recognize this?"

"Madison wore a bracelet like that Friday night," Debbie said.

"It's Madison's all right," Kim said. "I gave it to her."

CHAPTER SIX

*A*fter Debbie closed the café at two, cleaned, prepared for the next day, and then spent more time planning for the Fall-iday train rides, she stepped outside and locked the door behind her. She walked around to the patio behind the depot, where she and Janet had set tables in the summer. Beyond, a freight train slowly chugged by.

She turned toward the nearby neighborhood—her neighborhood. The late afternoon was crisp and clear, and the tree branches swayed a little in the breeze. As she crossed the tracks and headed out, a gust of wind shot up the street, tearing dry maple leaves from a massive tree ahead. They floated down, dropping in front of her. She stepped on one, feeling like a giddy child as it crunched under her boot.

Someone had a wood fire burning. She passed a flower garden with browning cosmos and zinnias. There was a beauty in the waning garden that delighted Debbie.

Her thoughts shifted from autumn to the bracelet Ian had found. Just because Madison's bracelet was discovered alongside the cabinet the model depot had been placed on didn't mean she had taken the depot. But why would the bracelet be there? Madison had it on when she was in the café on Friday night, before she, Jaxon, and Julian returned to the museum. The bracelet fell off her wrist, or was taken off, sometime after that. But how? Or why?

"Debbie!"

She turned. Kristy, leading a small terrier on a leash, waved.

Debbie waved back as Kristy hurried toward her.

"Who's your little one?" Debbie asked.

"BG, for Big Girl." Kristy grinned. "She doesn't realize she only weighs five pounds."

Debbie bent down and petted the dog. It gave a little bark and then licked her hand. "She's darling."

"Do you have a dog?" Kristy asked.

Debbie shook her head. Thankfully, Greg had Hammer, his border collie, and Janet had a Yorkie named Laddie, so Debbie could still get her dog fixes.

"Your mother told me about your fiancé," Kristy said. "Carson and I had no idea about what happened. I don't know how we missed that. I'm so sorry."

"Thank you," Debbie said.

"Do you have any plans for supper?" Kristy asked. "Carson's making dinner. Chicken parmesan."

"Sounds delicious."

"It will be. Carson's a marvelous cook." Kristy switched the leash to her other hand. "How about it?"

"Shouldn't you ask Carson first?" Debbie asked.

Kristy smiled. "I'll text him, but I know he won't mind." She pulled out her phone and sent a quick text. Her phone dinged almost immediately. She read aloud, "'That's a great idea. Tell Debbie I'm putting a third plate on the table right now.'" Kristy looked up from her phone and grinned. "What do you say?"

"Thank you. That's what I say." Debbie couldn't help but smile back at Kristy, whose grin was infectious. "What a treat to not have to go home and figure out dinner."

"Let's go." Kristy took a step forward.

"Does Carson cook dinner every day?"

"Pretty much," Kristy said. "He enjoys it much more than I do. When we lived in Chicago, takeout was my specialty, but there aren't as many options here."

"Where in Chicago did you live?"

"Right downtown, just a few blocks from the lake." She glanced down at the dog, who pranced along beside them with her head held high. "BG is definitely a city dog. She hasn't quite gotten used to living in a small town. We encountered a racoon the other night, which caused quite a scene. She acted as if it was a dragon."

Debbie could imagine.

They turned right in two blocks and then reached the Argyle place. Debbie had never been inside, but she certainly remembered it. The house was on a double lot. As they started up the driveway, she saw a building in the backyard beyond the detached garage. Perhaps it was a garden shed.

Kristy led the way through the back entrance and onto a mud porch, where they took off their boots.

Carson opened the door to the kitchen. "Welcome!" he said.

Kristy motioned for Debbie to go first, and as she stepped into the kitchen, she inhaled the savory scent of chicken, cheese, and tomato sauce. And was that chocolate? Yes, a platter of brownies sat on the counter.

Carson gave Debbie a hug and said, "How about a glass of seltzer?"

"Yes, please," Debbie said.

Kristy let the dog off the leash, and BG pranced into the kitchen and went straight to her bed in the far corner of the room.

As Carson headed to the refrigerator, Debbie's gaze drifted to the dining room. The table was set for three with china, crystal, and cloth napkins.

Carson handed her a glass of seltzer. "I'm just getting ready to dish up. Kristy, would you get the salad out of the refrigerator?"

As Kristy washed her hands, Debbie asked, "What can I do to help?"

"I'll hand you the bread," Carson said. "You can put it in the basket."

Debbie washed her hands after Kristy finished. Out the kitchen window, she had a view of the backyard. "What an adorable building." It clearly wasn't a garden shed. There were windows and a light was on. She turned toward her hosts as she dried her hands.

Carson smiled. "We use it as an office." Kristy took the salad to the table without comment.

"That's one of the things that convinced us to move here— enough office space for both of us," Carson said. "We were a bit cramped in Chicago."

Debbie imagined Kristy had a lot of meetings and collaborative work, all online. She'd ask to see the office later.

After a fabulous meal and brownies à la mode, Debbie excused herself to use the bathroom. She saw that all the doors in the hallway were closed. Neither Kristy nor Carson offered to give her a tour of the house, and she didn't ask. Besides the rooms off the hallway, there was also the upstairs and the detached garage, not to mention the office in the backyard.

The conversation mostly centered around the work they'd done to the house before they moved in.

"We painted everything, of course, and put down new flooring," Kristy said.

"Next, we're going to do the kitchen. The last time Mom and Dad remodeled, we were all in middle school." Carson laughed.

It didn't seem that long ago to Debbie but, of course, it was.

"We won't do that for a few months though, maybe in the spring," Carson said. "When I can barbecue and won't have to cook everything on a hot plate in the dining room. Do you know of any good contractors in town?"

"Greg Connor. You met him yesterday at church."

Carson leaned back against the sofa. "I'm guessing he has a good reputation."

"The best," Debbie said. "He flips houses but also does other work. He did my house. You might talk with him."

"Great," Carson said.

Debbie took out her phone. "What's your number? I'll share his with you."

Once Debbie had Carson's number, she sent him Greg's.

Next, they talked about classmates, although Kristy didn't contribute much to that conversation. Debbie asked Carson if he had any family left in Dennison since his parents moved away.

"I think I told you, my sister and her family live in Cleveland, which was why Mom and Dad went there. I have a few distant cousins but no one I'm close to, except for my aunt."

"Oh, that's so nice you have her." Debbie's grandparents had passed away by the time she was a teenager. Perhaps that was one of the reasons she treasured elderly people so much. Or, more likely, her father's job as director of Good Shepherd for all those years was a big reason she liked old people. She'd grown up with them. "Does she live in a care center?"

He shook his head. "She's still in her home. She keeps busy at the senior center—bingo, bridge, even aerobics. She volunteers around town some. I check in on her once a week, but she doesn't need much help."

After they'd finished their coffee, Debbie thanked both of them. "I've had a wonderful time," she said. "May I help clean the kitchen?"

"No." Kristy smiled. "That's my job. Carson cooks, and I clean."

Debbie was beginning to think she'd imagined Kristy's issues in high school. She seemed so centered and personable now.

"Well, thank you," she said. "I really appreciate your hospitality."

"I'll walk you out," Kristy said. Debbie followed her through the kitchen toward the back porch where her boots were. She'd ask to see the office some other time. She didn't want to overstay her welcome.

BG woke up and toddled out of her bed and across the kitchen floor. Debbie bent down and scratched the dog's head and then continued to the back porch, where she put on her boots.

"Do you want me to walk with you?" Kristy asked. "I wouldn't mind."

"Oh no," Debbie said. "I'll be fine. It's only a few blocks."

She started down the outside steps.

When she reached the driveway, she realized Kristy was behind her. "I'm not quite sure how to say this," Kristy said, "but I want to apologize for my behavior our last years of high school."

Caught off guard, all Debbie could manage to say was, "Oh?"

Kristy wrapped her arms around herself. "Honestly, there's a lot I can't remember from the end of high school, but I did remember after I saw you Friday night at the depot that you were always very kind to me. And I didn't reciprocate that, even though we were good friends before."

"Thank you," Debbie said. "Our friendship did change those last two years. Now, looking back, I'm guessing you were going through something difficult."

Kristy dipped her head but didn't offer any more information. "Anyway," she said, "you've been so kind and welcoming to me. I appreciate it."

Debbie leaned toward Kristy. "It's really nice to have you back in Dennison. I hope we get to spend more time together."

"Thank you." Kristy dropped her hands to her sides. "I think I'll come into the café tomorrow on my morning break and get a cup of coffee. I get more work done in the long run if I get out of the house for a bit."

"Sounds good," Debbie said. "And I'd love to hear more about your work."

Kristy waved her hand dismissively.

Debbie gave Kristy a quick hug. "See you tomorrow."

She quickened her pace when she reached the street. Mom, of course, had been right that Kristy was going through difficulties toward the end of high school. If only Debbie had listened to her all those years ago.

Debbie thought about Kristy remembering that she hadn't been kind to Debbie. Did she remember that she'd stolen Debbie's favorite earrings?

As she neared her house, Debbie's phone rang. *Ray.* She accepted the call. "Hello, Ray."

"Debbie?" His voice sounded unsteady. "I can't find the painting of the depot I showed you on Saturday. Did I take it back to my room?"

"Yes," Debbie said.

"It's supposed to be on my bookcase, on the top shelf. But it's not there."

"Maybe it's somewhere else in your room."

"I've looked everywhere. So has Gayle. Neither of us can find it."

"Did someone else pick it up by accident?" Debbie knew, from Dad being the director of Good Shepherd for all those years, that all sorts of things went missing there. Usually, it was that someone had set something down and then someone else picked it up and put it somewhere else. It was like playing hide-and-seek with objects instead of people.

"No, we've looked and looked."

"We can use the photo I took and make flyers. Maybe the image will jog someone's memory," Debbie said. "I'll be right there."

Debbie always enjoyed going to the Good Shepherd Retirement Center in the evening, even when she was a young girl. The stained-glass window of Jesus with the lamb in His arms was backlit and gave the image an even softer look than during the day.

Jesus had said, *"Let the little children come to me, and do not hinder them, for the kingdom of heaven belongs to such as these."* She believed He felt the same about the elderly, who were often children at heart. In fact, James wrote that true religion was to look after widows and orphans in their distress. Not all widows were elderly, but so many of the elderly were widows—or widowers.

The murmur from the last of the residents in the dining hall and the clatter from the kitchen also brought comfort. When Debbie was a girl, most of the residents knew her, and she'd often have a bowl of ice cream at one of the tables with a group as she waited for Dad to finish up his work. Some of the residents didn't have children in their lives, and their contact with her and the children of other staff was the only interaction they had with young people.

No one was at the front counter again, so Debbie signed in as a visitor and then headed straight for Ray's door, which was wide open. She knocked anyway, and a woman said, "Come on in."

Gayle sat on Ray's couch while he rummaged inside his closet, his wheelchair in as far as it would go. She smiled. "Hello."

Ray popped his head out of the closet. "Hi, Debbie," he said, pushing the wheelchair back. "Thank you for coming."

"Of course. I'm so sorry the painting is missing." She held up her phone. "I'll go track down the receptionist and see if she can print out some flyers. I'm sure it will turn up."

"I hope so," Ray said. "I keep thinking I must have moved it, but I've looked everywhere. Three times now."

"Sit tight," Debbie said. "I'll return ASAP."

She headed back to the front counter and rang the bell. When no one responded, she stuck her head in the dining hall. Eileen sat at a table with a younger woman. Debbie started toward them.

"What are you doing here?" Eileen asked.

"I'm on a special assignment," Debbie responded.

"No doubt." Eileen introduced Debbie to the young woman and then said, "This is Ashley Cramer. She's our new receptionist."

"I'm so pleased to meet you." Debbie sat down next to Eileen and across from Ashley. "You're just the person I wanted to see."

Ashley tilted her head. "Oh?"

Debbie explained the situation with Ray's missing painting. "I was hoping we could make a flyer and print out a few to post around the center."

Ashley frowned. "I haven't done a flyer here."

"I can do it on my phone," Debbie said. "I'll just need to print them."

"All right..."

"It's a wireless printer." Debbie stood. "I might need the password, if it's been changed recently." Debbie used to make flyers for her dad.

Ashley gave her a questioning look. Before Debbie could explain, Eileen said, "Debbie's father, Vance Albright, was the director here. He retired recently."

"Oh." Ashley stood. "I'm new to Dennison. It's taking me a while to put together all the connections."

Eileen stood too. "I'm going to go check on Ray. Is Gayle still here?"

"Yes," Debbie said. "I'll be down in a few minutes. But I'll show you the painting first." She pulled up the picture of the painting on her phone.

Eileen squinted. "Oh, that's what's missing? That little, odd painting of Ray's?"

Debbie nodded. "That's the one."

"I was surprised he'd saved it after the move."

Debbie wasn't. She rather liked the painting. "Do you think there's any chance Marguerite painted it?"

Eileen wrinkled her nose. "No doubt Marguerite could have painted whatever she wanted to, but I never saw anything of that style in her portfolio." She waved. "See you in a few minutes."

As Eileen turned toward the sitting room, Debbie followed Ashley to the reception area. She opened her app to design the flyer as she walked. By the time they reached the counter, she'd uploaded the picture of the painting. Then she added text, asking anyone who had information to contact Ray in Room 157 or call Debbie Albright, with her number included.

She pushed save, titled the document, and said, "Done."

"Wow," Ashley said. "I'm impressed."

"I co-own the Whistle Stop Café at the depot," Debbie explained. "Marketing doesn't come naturally to me, but this was an easy task." She tapped on the printer icon, and the center's device popped up, but when she tried to print, nothing happened. She looked up at Ashley. "It must have a new password. Do you know what it is?"

Ashley sat down at the desk behind the counter and logged on to the computer. "Let me look it up in my training manual." She clicked a few times and turned her screen so Debbie could see. "Here it is."

Debbie typed the password into her phone, and it connected to the printer. "I'm in." She specified five copies and then hit print. The printer came on and began to spurt out the pages.

Ashley walked over to it, collected the copies, and put them on the counter in front of Debbie. "Now I know who to contact if I'm asked to make any flyers."

Debbie smiled as Ashley opened a drawer on the other side of the counter and pulled out a roll of tape.

The clock on the far wall read seven forty-five. "Do you get off at eight?" Debbie asked.

Ashley nodded.

Debbie picked up the tape and flyers. "Well, if you're gone before I'm done, have a good evening." She headed back to the dining room. She posted the first flyer on the right-hand side of the doors where everyone could see it.

She posted the second in the sitting area and the third by the elevator. Next, she took the elevator up to the second floor and posted a flyer in the sitting area there too.

Once she returned to the first floor, she headed to Ray's room to give him the last flyer in case there was somewhere specific he wanted it posted.

"Thank you," Ray said.

"Hopefully you'll have it back by morning, and you can tell me what happened tomorrow at dinner." Debbie turned to Gayle. "Does six o'clock work?"

"Perfectly. I'll tell Eileen—she was just here—and we'll leave at five forty-five."

Which meant they'd most likely arrive at Debbie's by five fifty. She needed to stop by the store on the way home.

On her way out of the center, Debbie stopped at the counter to sign out. As she did, she glanced at the visitors for the day. She recognized two of the names. *Dylan Rhodes* and *Madison Palmer.* What in the world? She read the time. Both signed in at one fifteen with "volunteer" as the reason. But there was no sign-out time.

Debbie looked around for Ashley to see if she remembered Madison or Dylan being at Good Shepherd that afternoon, but it appeared Ashley had already left. It was 8:05.

Madison's great-grandmother lived at Good Shepherd, so Debbie understood her reasons to be there. But why would Dylan be volunteering at the assisted living center? And if he wasn't, what other reason could he have to be there?

Most importantly, did either one of them know anything about the missing painting?

CHAPTER SEVEN

T he next morning, as Paulette worked the floor and Debbie helped fill the orders, Janet began singing "Happy Birthday" to Debbie.

Debbie groaned as she placed a biscuit on a plate along with a pat of butter. "Don't make me older than I am. I have ten days until my birthday."

Janet grinned. "I know, old lady." Janet's birthday wasn't until July, so Debbie was a few months older, a fact she good-naturedly pointed out once in a while.

"So do you have plans for your birthday?" Janet asked.

"Just dinner and cake with my parents," Debbie said. "Nothing spectacular."

Debbie picked up the food and headed out to the floor to the first table, where Harry and Patricia sat talking. Crosby, Harry's trusty canine, sat at his owner's feet. Patricia ordered her usual peppermint mocha and pastry, and Harry ordered a hearty breakfast—fried eggs, bacon, home fries, and toast.

"Here you go," Debbie said as she set the plates in front of them. "I'll be right back with more coffee."

A few minutes later, as Debbie started a new pot of coffee, Kristy came through the door of the café. Again, she wore a stylish sweater.

This one was camel colored and tunic length. Was it cashmere? Debbie hadn't seen Kristy wear the same color twice in the last five days. She noted her boots. Yep, she hadn't seen those before either. Debbie guessed by the way Kristy dressed that she had worked in a downtown office when she lived in Chicago.

"Good morning," Debbie called out.

"Hi!" Kristy had a bounce to her step as she headed for the counter. When she saw Janet, she waved.

Debbie grabbed a mug. "I'm guessing you're here for that cup of coffee."

"Yes ma'am." Kristy sat down on a stool. "And how about a pastry too? What do you recommend?"

"Janet's toffee apple tart." Debbie began pouring the coffee. "Definitely. In fact, you should have two, which will be two fewer than I'll eat by the end of the day."

Kristy laughed. "I'll take one—it sounds delicious."

Debbie set the full mug on the counter in front of Kristy and plated the tart just as Janet came out of the kitchen.

For the moment, traffic had slowed in the café. Janet poured herself a cup of coffee and came around the end of the counter and sat next to Kristy.

"I think it's so fun that the two of you work together." Kristy cut into her tart. "You were always so close. How cool that you've created this exceptional space for the community." She took a bite of the tart. "Wow!" She swallowed. "This is delicious." She turned to Janet. "I remember you used to bake in high school. You always made everyone cakes for their birthdays."

Janet smiled. "I loved doing that."

"Speaking of..." Kristy spun on her stool to address Debbie. "Your birthday is coming up, isn't it? On the twentieth, right?"

Debbie shook her head. "I can't believe you remember the date."

Kristy put her fork down. "Oh, those are the things I do remember. It's the other important things I can't seem to recall." She took a sip of her coffee and then said, "So how will you celebrate?"

"I'm just having dinner and cake with my parents."

"That sounds lovely." Kristy suddenly sat up straighter. "Oh, I have an idea. How about you all come over for a party at our house? Carson can cook. I'll decorate." She turned to Janet. "Would you make a cake? For old time's sake?"

"Definitely," Janet said.

Kristy faced Debbie again. "What do you say?"

Debbie pursed her lips. "That I need to check with my mother?" They all laughed.

"Well, let me know what they say." Kristy looked as if she might explode from excitement. "And we can talk about who else to invite too."

"That all sounds lovely," Debbie said. "Give me a day to think about it and talk to Mom. I'll get back to you."

"Just let me know by the beginning of next week. That will give us plenty of time." Kristy took another bite of the tart and sighed. "Really, this is amazing."

Debbie hoped they'd figure out who took the model depot by her birthday. Surely whoever the culprit was would be uncovered by then, wouldn't they?

After the lunch rush ended and before Janet left for home, Debbie headed down to the museum to talk with Kim. Usually, Kim stopped in at the café in the morning or at least by noon. Maybe she was extra busy today.

She hoped the reason Kim hadn't stopped in wasn't because she didn't want to talk about Madison's bracelet, because that was exactly what Debbie did want to talk about. And about Ray's missing painting.

When Debbie arrived at the museum, Carson, who held a legal pad in his hands, was talking with Kim.

"Let's go outside and look at the train car while we talk," Kim suggested as Carson waved at Debbie. Kim turned. "Oh, hi. Do you have a question for me?"

"I do," Debbie said. "But it can wait. I'll come down after the café closes."

"Aren't we going to go to Ray's with Sofia then?"

"We need to postpone that. Ray's painting is missing."

"What happened?"

"We don't know. But could you call Sofia and let her know?"

"Yes." Kim nodded. "See you later, then."

Carson gave Debbie a questioning look. Not wanting to say anything more, she just smiled at him and went back to the café. Paulette had left, and Janet was getting ready to go too. "Are you ready for your dinner party tonight?" Janet asked.

"I think so. I have my shopping done," Debbie said. "I need to chop the vegetables and put them and the chicken on to roast when I get home."

"Do you have dessert?"

"Shortbread and herbal tea." Debbie grinned. "Simple and safe."

"You should take what's left of the toffee apple tarts. I have enough ingredients to make more in the morning." Janet pointed to the fridge. "I left a list of what else I need for the rest of the week."

"Perfect," Debbie said. "I'll do the shopping tomorrow."

A few minutes later, after the last customer left and Debbie had flipped the sign, Kim opened the door. "Am I too late?"

"Of course not," Debbie said. "I haven't dumped the coffee yet. And I have one of Janet's toffee apple tarts, just for you. On the house."

Kim exhaled. "You're so good to me. Thank you."

"I'll have a cup of coffee and a tart too." Debbie grinned and motioned to the first table. "Sit. I'll join you in a jiffy."

After she plated the tarts and poured the coffee, she put everything on a tray and took it out to the table.

Kim was on her phone but put it down. "Thank goodness Tony is getting back this afternoon. Barry and I are too old to parent a teenager. Madison will go home after her volleyball practice."

Debbie put a cup of coffee and the treat in front of Kim. "What did Madison say about the bracelet?"

"That it's hers but she doesn't know how it got there. She said the last time she was aware of the bracelet was that night in the cafe," Kim said. "She picked up a napkin that had fallen behind the cabinet, and she wonders if the bracelet fell off then."

That sounded like a poor excuse to Debbie, but she didn't say so.

After Debbie put her coffee and tart on the table and the tray on the counter, Kim said, "When she was getting ready for bed that night, she realized it was gone."

"But she didn't say anything?" Debbie asked.

"She didn't." Kim picked up her fork and took a bite. "Mmm, delicious. Where did Janet get this recipe?"

Debbie smiled. "She won't tell me."

Kim took another bite and then a sip of coffee. "I think it's more likely Jaxon took the model depot."

Debbie was surprised but didn't respond. None of the evidence so far pointed toward Jaxon.

"When I picked Madison up at school yesterday, he was waiting with her," Kim said. "He's obviously smitten. What if he took her ridiculous statement seriously? And did you notice on Saturday, when Ian was talking with everyone, that Julian spoke for both of them and that Jaxon didn't deny taking the model depot?"

Debbie had noticed that. "What about Dylan?"

Kim shook her head. "He doesn't have any reason to try to impress Madison. She's already crazy about him. That's the problem. Besides, he left and didn't come back. No one saw him after he said goodbye."

Debbie didn't say anything, but Dylan could have sneaked in while they were cleaning.

Kim sighed. "I should probably just commission someone to make a new depot. Do you think Greg would do it?"

"I don't know," Debbie said. "I imagine it would take a bit of time to get it right, with the dimensions and all, don't you think?"

Kim shrugged.

"You said earlier you might ask one of the volunteers," Debbie said. "Don't they usually make repairs and repaint and add new buildings and trees and tunnels and things like that?"

"Usually," Kim said. "But the depot will definitely be more complicated. I'll ask one of them tomorrow."

Debbie took another sip of coffee. "Maybe you should wait a bit longer and see if it turns up."

"I don't know." Kim sighed. "It's already been four days. Seems like whoever took it isn't going to bring it back."

"Let's not give up." Debbie pondered her short list. "It could still be returned any time." Madison could have it. Or Dylan. Or Jaxon. As much as she didn't want it to be true, Jaxon could have taken it, put it in his football bag, and then hidden it somewhere at home.

Debbie decided to change the subject. "I wanted to talk more about Ray's missing painting."

"I let Sofia know."

"Thank you." Debbie tucked a strand of hair behind her ear. "When I stopped by Good Shepherd last night, I noticed Madison's name on the visitor register for yesterday afternoon. And Dylan's."

Kim had a puzzled expression on her face.

"They signed in at one fifteen."

Kim's face lit up. "Right. I remember now." An expression of relief settled on her face. "They both volunteer at the care center on Mondays, Wednesdays, and Fridays, from one thirty to two thirty for one of their classes. I don't know what he does, but Madison facilitates an exercise class in the common area on the first floor. She leads them in exercises they can do from a chair. Mom loves it."

That area was right outside Ray's room. Debbie toyed with her mug. "How does she get to the care center from the high school?" It was a couple of miles.

"She rides with Dylan. That's how they got to know each other. I think it's called Career Class or something like that."

"Interesting."

Kim tilted her head and sighed. "I'll ask Madison about the painting, because obviously you think she took it and the depot."

"No," Debbie said. "I don't think she took either, but I think it's worth noting that she had an opportunity to take both. Maybe it's coincidental…"

Debbie wouldn't add that maybe it wasn't. Or that Dylan would have had a chance to take the painting too.

At five fifty, Debbie turned the oven to warm and walked to the living room as a car door slammed outside. The trio had arrived.

She opened the front door and hurried out onto the porch and down the steps. She'd moved the pumpkins and cornstalks to the back of the porch by the outdoor furniture, wanting a wide path for her elderly guests. "Good evening!" she called out.

Eileen was on the sidewalk, moving toward the house, while Gayle stood at the passenger door with Ray's wheelchair in place.

Debbie headed straight for him as he stood and transferred himself into the chair. "How is everyone tonight?"

"Just fine," Ray replied.

"Sad it's my last day in Dennison," Gayle answered.

"Aw," Debbie replied. "I'll be sorry to have you go."

"So will I," Ray said. "I wish you'd consider moving here."

Gayle patted his shoulder. "Sometimes I do."

Eileen led the way up the steps, using the railing, and Gayle followed while Debbie pushed Ray up the ramp to the side of the porch stairs.

"Go on in," Debbie told Eileen as she reached the porch. "It's open." By the time they were all inside, Eileen had her jacket hanging on one of the hooks alongside the built-in bench and Gayle was already in the middle of the living room.

"Look at the box ceiling," Gayle said. "You did such a good job restoring the wood."

"I wish I could take credit," Debbie answered. "But Greg Connor, with my dad's help, did the work."

"It's gorgeous," Gayle said.

"Let me take your sweater," Debbie said to her. "And then I'll give you the tour." She turned to Eileen and Ray. "Do you two want to join us?"

Ray shook his head. "I've seen it all recently." Debbie knew the stairs were nearly impossible for him. He could walk short distances but going up and down a steep staircase was a challenge.

"I'll stay here with Ray," Eileen said.

"Make yourselves comfortable," Debbie said. "We won't be long." She led the way through the dining room and into the kitchen.

"It smells delicious," Gayle said. "And it all looks so nice. The new cabinets. The new flooring." She turned back toward the dining room. "But I'm glad you kept the old hardwood floors."

"Oh, I wouldn't have changed those for the world. They make the house." Debbie lowered her voice. "The flooring in here had some water damage."

"Oh, I know," Gayle said. "I told Ray to get that fixed, over and over."

Next Debbie led the way upstairs, first to the main bedroom. "This used to be Mama and Papa's room," Gayle said.

"That's what Ray told me." Debbie headed down the hallway to the second bedroom. "I haven't done much of anything with this room. Would you still like to see it?"

"Absolutely," Gayle said. "It was my room." When they entered, she said, "Actually, this used to be two rooms. My father knocked out the wall after I got married and moved out. Both rooms were like walk-in closets." She laughed. "It was plenty big enough for us back then, but everyone wants bigger rooms now."

"Well," Debbie said, "this house is perfect for me."

Gayle beamed. "It is."

When they got back to the living room, Debbie took ahold of Ray's wheelchair. "You all can go ahead and sit down." She pushed Ray toward the dining room. "I just need to get the chicken and vegetables from the kitchen." She'd made roasted chicken, acorn squash, and vegetables—potatoes, carrots, broccolini, and onions—on the side. A green salad and a loaf of rosemary bread completed the meal, along with the shortbread and the toffee apple tarts for dessert.

"Ray, I'm putting you at the head of the table. And, Gayle, you sit opposite him. Eileen and I will sit on the sides." Debbie had an orange tablecloth with a leaf-patterned runner on the table. In the middle, she'd arranged several miniature pumpkins and gourds around three floating orange candles in rose bowls.

"What a lovely table," Eileen said.

Debbie thanked her and headed into the kitchen. She'd bought the dining room set after Reed had proposed, dreaming of the two of them and their children—boys, girls, one of each, she didn't care!—sitting around it. She shook her head as she opened the oven door. Funny how those memories popped up at the most unexpected times.

She carried the platter of chicken and acorn squash with browned butter in one hand and the platter of vegetables in the other and placed them on the hot pads on the table runner.

Debbie led the group in prayer and then dished up everyone's plates. They passed around the green salad and bread.

Toward the end of the meal, Gayle said, "I can't tell you how much I'm enjoying being in your home. Thank you for taking such good care of it and loving it like our parents did all those years ago." She smiled at Ray. "And the way my brother did too."

"How kind of you. That means so much." Debbie was absolutely sincere. Gayle was as sweet and caring as Ray. It was obvious they were related.

As Debbie stood to clear the plates, she said, "Gayle, would you tell me what it was like for you here in Dennison during the war and soon after?"

"I'd love to."

"Let's move into the living room," Debbie said. "I'll bring dessert and tea in a few minutes."

CHAPTER EIGHT

Debbie started the tea, cleared the food from the table, and then put the dessert, plates, forks, and napkins on a tray. Once she had everything on the coffee table and served and everyone had oohed and aahed over Janet's tarts, Debbie asked Gayle what it was like to have her brother off to war.

"I'm seven years younger than Ray, so I was only eleven when he left," Gayle said. "It was an uncertain time, but I was so proud of him. And so determined to pray for him and do anything I could to support our country, just like everyone else I knew. Both Mama and Daddy worked at the depot, so I did as much cooking and gardening as I could. Mama and I would plan the meals for the week every Friday evening and then she would do the shopping, being careful with our rations. We had a large victory garden and canned everything we could in the fall. We kept a few chickens in the backyard for eggs and chicken stew a couple of times a year. We were a small family, just the three of us besides Ray, compared to some of the larger families around with seven or eight children.

"We were glued to the news. We listened to the radio every evening and pored over the newspaper. We lived for Ray's letters. Of course, he couldn't say much, and all sorts of things were redacted, things we could only guess at. But after D-Day, when we finally heard from him, we were so relieved. He'd survived! Then when the war in Europe ended, we were so relieved again—until we found out about his injury. But not knowing how severe it was, we weren't sure if he'd be sent to the Pacific or not. You can imagine how we felt on September 2, 1945, when Japan signed the surrender papers." Gayle wiped her eyes. "We knew he'd be coming home soon. It was quite the experience."

"For me too," Ray quipped.

They all laughed.

"What was life in Dennison like after the war?" Debbie asked Gayle.

"A lot like it was before the war but minus the worry. Which made all the difference. I mean, we never totally relaxed until Ray was home. We heard stories of soldiers and sailors dying after the war—infections, accidents, that sort of thing. As far as life here, troop trains were still coming through the station at a remarkable rate. German POW trains came through too, taking them to the East Coast to get on ships to Europe that also held supplies for rebuilding. Those ships brought soldiers stateside, who would get on trains to go to military bases to be decommissioned and then head home. Trains from the West Coast brought sailors home too. Our groceries, meat, nylons, and so much more were still rationed. I didn't own a pair of nylons until I was seventeen. No one could buy a new car or appliances. Factories had to be changed from making planes and ammunition to everyday items again."

"What did you do for fun?" Debbie asked.

"Pretty much the same things we did during the war." She grinned. "It wasn't all worry. Our parents loved to go to community dances, and I'd go with them. The music of the time was such a boost. I don't know what we would have done without it. We also had church potlucks and picnics in the summer. Occasionally, Father would give me a nickel to go to the movies with my friends. All the neighborhood kids would play baseball in a spare lot and get together in the evenings to play hide-and-seek before darkness fell. Growing up in Dennison was a joy."

"Who were some of your neighbors?" Debbie asked.

"Isn't it interesting how, as a kid, you don't know that much about the adults? And then when you get to be middle-aged and older you think about those adults more and wonder what their lives were really like and what they were going through at the time."

Debbie nodded. She was getting to the age where she was thinking about the parents of her classmates more, such as Kristy's mom and dad. One of the things she treasured was knowing Janet's parents, Steve and Lorilee, as an adult.

"Anyway," Gayle said, "families looked out for one another and for each other's kids. I was on my own after school, but I knew I could go to any of the other mothers in the neighborhood if I needed anything." She smiled. "But it was the other kids my age that I spent most of my time with. One of them was Minnie Jennings."

"Jennings? Any relationship to Bob, Marguerite, and Sofia Jennings?"

"Yes," Gayle said. "The same. Minnie was Bob's little sister. We bonded over both of us having brothers in the war. We supported each other and listened to each other's worries and prayed for Ray and Bob.

"I thought about this more after we talked about Marguerite the other day. That's how I got the babysitting job, because I was

friends with Minnie. When she was busy, I got to babysit Sofia."
Gayle paused for a moment and then said, "I was fascinated by
Marguerite. She was glamorous but in a natural way." She laughed.
"Is that possible?"

"I think so," Debbie said. "It sounds as if she didn't have to try.
Would that be right, Eileen?"

"Absolutely," Eileen said. "Some of the women in town seemed
to resent Marguerite and thought she was arrogant, but nothing was
further from the truth. She was focused. It wasn't as if she had a lot
of clothes, but what she had was quality, and she knew how to mix
and match them. Her hair was long, and she wore it in a French
twist for as long as I knew her. Her home was simple but elegant. She
was glamorous without trying. She had an Audrey Hepburn look to
her. Effortlessly lovely."

"I'd put Minnie in the camp of women who resented Marguerite."
Gayle turned to Eileen. "What do you remember?"

"I know many people thought that Bob marrying a Parisienne
and bringing her back was scandalous. Marguerite was only a year
older than Bob, but people spoke of her as an 'older woman,' and some
assumed she'd trapped him. Marguerite was elegant while Bob was
an all-American Midwestern young man. He'd played football in
high school, he loved to hunt, he worked as a carpenter. Nothing
about him was sophisticated. All of France had been in survival mode
for years. Everyone was at risk for different reasons. So many women
were left to fend for themselves, often against the occupying Germans,
especially in Paris. It was obvious that Marguerite had suffered in
ways those of us in America couldn't imagine. She didn't speak much
about her wartime experiences, but I got the idea she was involved

with the Resistance. I imagine Bob seemed like a haven of safety by the time she met him."

"Fascinating," Debbie said. "How did the rest of the Jennings family feel about Marguerite, besides Minnie?"

Gayle turned to Eileen. "You would know better than I would."

"Well," Eileen said, "I don't want to gossip, but I doubt Minnie came up with her thoughts on her own."

Gayle sighed. "I heard Minnie's mother complain about Marguerite too—about how odd she was, how aloof. How she hardly seemed a part of the family."

"What about Bob? What was he like?"

"Robert Jennings?" Eileen paused a moment. "He was a good, solid, simple man. The only negative thing I can say about him is that he never appreciated Marguerite's cooking the way he should have—like I did." Eileen laughed. "Not that he didn't enjoy it. He did. He just didn't know how lucky he was. But he appreciated everything else about her. And he stood up for her when it came to his family. It caused a bit of a rift. Sadly, Sofia was never very close to his people."

Gayle's eyes grew wide. "I just remembered something I haven't thought of for years. At the time it was a bit of a scandal. Perhaps it paved the way for more people to feel animosity toward Marguerite."

"What's that?" Debbie asked.

"There was another neighbor girl named Anna. Minnie and I hung out with her some after Ray and Bob were drafted."

"I don't remember an Anna in our neighborhood," Ray said.

"She was a year younger than you and didn't move to Dennison until the spring of your senior year," Gayle said. "Anna was six years older than we were, and now I wonder why she spent time with us. I think she must have been emotionally immature or something. She went on a few dates with Bob before he left, which was a couple of months after you did, Ray. Anna wrote letters to Bob, and he wrote her back, although not as often as she wrote him." Gayle clasped her hands together. "Then all of a sudden she stopped hearing from him."

Debbie froze, her cup halfway to her lips. "Was he injured?"

"No," Gayle said. "He'd married Marguerite."

"But he didn't write to tell Anna that?"

"He did eventually. Minnie was miffed with him. Anna was never kind to Marguerite, but by 1948 or '49, she had married. I used to see her from time to time way back when, sometimes with Minnie. Their mutual dislike of Marguerite seemed to unite them in an odd way."

"Is Minnie still alive?" Debbie asked.

"No." Gayle pursed her lips. "Minnie passed away twenty-plus years ago from cancer."

"What about Anna?"

"I don't know," Gayle answered. "I lost track of her after Minnie died. Like I said, I haven't thought of her in years, and I'm having a senior moment when it comes to her maiden name—and her married names. I think she was married twice." She tapped her chest a couple of times with her palm and chuckled. "I'll probably think of at least one of her last names, most likely her maiden name, in the middle of the night."

Debbie chuckled. "I have those moments too."

Fifteen minutes later, after she escorted them to the car, Debbie made sure Ray's seat belt clicked and then said goodbye one more time to all three of the beloved elders. She stepped away from the car and waved. As Gayle backed out of the driveway, Debbie climbed her porch steps and then turned around. The Lincoln Continental headed down the street, toward the depot. Debbie went into the house.

She'd started toward the kitchen to load the dishwasher when she heard a crash and then metal scraping on metal. She froze for a moment and then spun around and dashed out of the house. Someone had just been in a car accident.

She hoped it wasn't Eileen, Ray, and Gayle.

Down the street, at the railroad crossing, two sets of headlights were askew. Debbie took her phone from her pocket and called 911 as she ran. Ahead, a young man climbed from a pickup truck in the intersection.

Another person was in the street. Someone called out, "Is everyone okay?" Debbie recognized that voice. Harry.

She ran faster. The scene came into focus. The pickup and a car—a Lincoln Continental—had collided. Debbie felt ill. Maybe Gayle shouldn't still be driving. The back passenger door of the car opened.

Eileen.

The 911 dispatcher answered the call. "There's been a wreck—a car and a pickup," Debbie said and gave the cross streets. "Please send an ambulance. There are three elderly people involved."

Harry, with Crosby at his side, beat her to the car and helped Eileen out. Still on the phone, Debbie opened Ray's door.

"Gayle." Ray, pushed back in the seat by the airbag, had his hand on his sister's shoulder. "Gayle, are you all right?"

Shattered glass from the windshield covered the airbags. Gayle's head was turned toward the driver's window and slumped against her shoulder. Blood trickled along her right temple, but it seemed to be coming from her forehead.

"What is the condition of the passengers?" the dispatcher asked.

"Two in the car are conscious. One is not." Debbie stepped back and looked up. The young man was now at the passenger door of the pickup, trying to open it. "Madison," he yelled. "Kick against the door."

"Madison?" Eileen stood beside Debbie. "Is that my Madison?"

"Madison!" the young man yelled again.

"Ma'am," the dispatcher said, "are you still there?"

"Yes. There seems to be an unresponsive person in the pickup too."

Harry put his arm around Eileen. "I'm going to take Eileen to my yard. If you think Ray can be moved, I have a chair for him too."

"All right," Debbie said.

"Harry, I need to go see about Madison first," Eileen said. "Will you help me over there?"

"Yes, of course," he said. "As long as it's safe. If it's dangerous, we'll need to hightail it out of there." The two started to shuffle around the back of the car, with Crosby following right behind them.

The dispatcher spoke again. "The police are on the way, and an ambulance has been notified. Is there any danger of the vehicles catching fire?"

"The damage is on the front passenger side of the pickup and the front driver side of the car," Debbie explained. "I don't think the gas tanks would be affected. The car is steaming under the hood."

"All right. Move the passengers if possible unless there's even a remote possibility of neck or back injuries. Of course, if either vehicle catches on fire, move all the passengers immediately."

"Thank you," Debbie said.

"Would you like me to stay on the line?"

Debbie heard sirens. "No," she said. "I can hear emergency vehicles already."

As she ended the call, Ray continued to say, "Gayle, can you hear me?"

Debbie thought her heart might break for the siblings. "Ray, the police are almost here, and the ambulance will be right behind them. Let's get you over to Harry's yard."

He shook his head. "I need to stay here with Gayle." His hand still rested on his sister's shoulder.

"All right," Debbie said. "I'll stay right here, beside you." She reached for his other hand.

"Madison!" Eileen shouted, her voice raw and loud. Then she turned toward the young man. "Why is my great-grandbaby with you?"

Debbie squinted. It was Dylan, the young man who was at the depot with Madison on Friday, the one who had asked her to homecoming. Above the wail of the siren, she heard him say to Eileen, "We were out for a ride is all." He climbed back in on the driver's side and pulled Madison toward him. Then he kicked the passenger door a couple of times, and it flew open as the police car arrived and the siren stopped.

Debbie had never been so relieved to see Ian in all her life.

"Madison." Eileen stepped forward and put her hand on Madison's face.

The girl began to stir. "Grammy? What happened?"

A half hour later, EMTs had loaded both Madison and Gayle, who had regained consciousness when the police arrived, into two ambulances. Eileen called Madison's father, Tony, and he arrived at the scene. He now sat on the curb beside Dylan, but Debbie couldn't hear what the two said. After a couple of minutes, Tony stood and approached Eileen and Debbie.

"Did Madison have permission to be out with him?" Eileen asked.

Tony shook his head. He looked as if he might cry. "I'm going to follow the ambulance."

Both Eileen and Ray were shaken up but seemed to be all right. Debbie insisted they go to the hospital to be checked out.

"I need to go to the hospital to see Gayle anyway," Ray said.

"And I need to go see Madison," Eileen added.

"I agree with Debbie that you should be checked out in the ER," Ian said. "Do you feel up to giving a statement first?" Ian took out his notebook. He nodded toward Dylan, who sat on the curb. "I'll talk with the owner of the pickup after I talk with both of you."

"Gayle was driving through the intersection," Ray said, "crossing the tracks, when the owner of the pickup turned left, without signaling. The two vehicles collided. I have to say, it seemed the driver of the pickup was going pretty fast. He wasn't there—and then suddenly he was."

Ian finished writing. "Eileen, what did you see?"

"The back of Ray's seat. Gayle was driving along at a very reasonable speed, and—smack—we were hit."

Ian made more notes. "Thank you." Then he looked up and said, "Two more ambulances are on their way."

"I'll go get my car so I can follow them to the hospital," Debbie said.

"Crosby and I will keep an eye on Ray and Eileen," Harry said.

"Thank you." Debbie headed toward the sidewalk. As she turned back toward her house, she overheard Dylan say to Ian, "I signaled to turn, and the car sped up and plowed into me, on Madison's side..."

Debbie felt ill again. She'd assumed Gayle was at fault when she came upon the accident, but she trusted Ray's testimony. Could Dylan not remember what happened? Or was he hoping to blame the accident on an elderly woman?

CHAPTER NINE

ednesday morning, Debbie left Janet and Paulette to run the café and headed straight to the hospital, where Gayle had been admitted. She'd finally convinced both Ray and Eileen, after the ER doctor cleared them, to go back to Good Shepherd at midnight. Madison had been in shock from the accident but was otherwise all right, except for a mild concussion. She'd been released, and her father had taken her home.

Gayle had a gash on her head and a broken wrist. She was having a CT scan when Ray finally agreed to leave. Gayle had listed Debbie as a contact so she could relay information to Ray as needed.

Debbie wanted to see how Gayle was before taking Ray back up to the hospital. To her shock, when she arrived, Madison sat in the waiting room.

"Madison." Debbie took a step toward her. "What are you doing here?"

"I couldn't sit still. I keep thinking about Gayle. And Ray. And Grammy. And what could have happened."

"Does your father know you're here?"

"No. He was in the shower when I left. He thinks I'm still in bed."

"Do you have your phone?"

She nodded.

"Call him and tell him you're here. Tell him I'll give you a ride home."

"All right," Madison said. "But I don't want to leave until I know how Gayle is."

Madison called her father. From Madison's side of the conversation, Debbie guessed he was upset and rightly so.

"Debbie will give me a ride home," Madison said. There was a long pause. "Okay. See you soon." She ended the call. "He's coming to get me."

Debbie knew that was best. She stood. "I'll see what I can find out about Gayle."

She walked to the nurses' station.

A nurse whose name tag read KELLY greeted her, and Debbie explained she was a contact for Gayle. "How's she doing?" Debbie asked. "I'm going to go see her brother and let him know."

"She's awake and alert. Her scan showed a concussion. Because she lost consciousness, we'll need to monitor her. She also needs a pin in her wrist. Hopefully, she can have the surgery this afternoon."

"Have you talked to her daughter?"

Kelly nodded. "There were quite a few conversations last night and again this morning. She's on her way. Gayle is well loved."

Debbie didn't doubt that. "She's a very lovable person."

"Absolutely," Kelly said.

"Can I bring her brother up to visit her today?"

"Yes," Kelly said. "But wait until after ten. And only stay for ten minutes. Her daughter should be here by then, so he can see her too."

By the time Debbie returned to the waiting room, Tony had arrived and was sitting across from Madison. He held her phone in his hands, probably because she wasn't supposed to use any screens as she healed. She sat with her arms crossed.

"Gayle is doing well," Debbie said. "They're keeping her so they can monitor her concussion, and she needs surgery on her wrist. I'll bring Ray to see her this morning."

"Will he be at the center this afternoon?" Madison asked. "Because I'll be there. I hope I can see him."

Tony shook his head. "You're staying home today."

"I'm fine."

"You have a concussion."

Madison stared at the floor. "A mild one."

"You may have lost consciousness."

"I didn't." She met her father's gaze. "I was frozen or something until I saw Grammy Eileen."

Tony clenched his jaw, appearing as if he was forcing himself not to speak. Debbie imagined he'd already said enough about Madison sneaking out last night and was trying not to repeat himself.

"Well," Debbie said. "I'm going to go get Ray."

Madison began to cry. "I want to see Grammy Eileen."

"We're going home," Tony said. "Chief Shaw is coming over to question you."

Madison shook her head. "I can't remember anything."

"Then tell him that." Tony stood. "Let's go."

When Debbie returned to the hospital with Ray, a woman who appeared to be in her late sixties greeted them in the waiting room. "Uncle Ray! Are you all right?"

"I'm fine." He dismissed her concern with a wave. "Trudy, I'd like you to meet Debbie Albright. She's the new owner of the old Zink place. Debbie, this is my niece, Trudy."

"It's a pleasure to meet you," Debbie said. "How's your mom doing?"

"Better, it seems," Trudy answered. "She's alert for being ninety-one and having a concussion. She feels horrible for causing the accident."

"She didn't cause the accident," Ray said. Debbie wondered if Gayle even remembered what happened. Perhaps she assumed she caused it.

Trudy raised her eyebrows.

"The pickup turned without signaling." Ray rubbed the back of his neck. "He came out of nowhere."

Trudy sighed. "That's good to know. I guess I assumed she was at fault."

Ray shook his head with his hand still on his neck. "She's a good driver. Even her nighttime driving."

"Mom doesn't remember speaking with an officer last night, and it doesn't sound as if anyone has talked with her this morning. I need to contact the insurance company and would like to have as much information as possible. Do you know the name of the driver of the pickup?"

Debbie glanced at Ray. He shrugged. "He's a high school student," Debbie said. "You should speak with Chief Shaw about him."

"I'll look into getting the police report," Trudy said. She turned to Ray. "Do you want to go see Mom? She's been asking for you."

"Absolutely." He rubbed his neck again.

"Are you sure you're all right, Uncle Ray?" Trudy asked.

He nodded. "Just a little sore. But those airbags are really something. It's not like the old days when I would have cracked my forehead on the dashboard."

Trudy agreed. "Well, I think you're doing amazing. It could have been so much worse."

A half hour later, Debbie took Ray back to the care center and headed to the grocery store to pick up the supplies Janet needed. When she returned to the café, Harry was sitting at the counter.

He smiled as Debbie carried in a box of supplies. "Need some help?"

She shook her head. "Thank you, but I only have one more box." She kept going to the kitchen.

Janet turned away from the grill. "How's Gayle doing?"

"All right. Her daughter, Trudy, is here, so that's good. The nurse told me Gayle will have surgery on her wrist this afternoon." Debbie put the box on the kitchen counter. "Trudy was wondering if anyone from the police department would talk to Gayle about the accident."

"I'd imagine so. Ian might stop by here this afternoon if he has a few extra minutes. You can ask him then."

After Debbie brought the second box in, she sat down next to Harry. "How are you after our late night?"

"Still a little shaken," he answered. "There have been a few accidents at that intersection over the years, but none involving people my age." His brown eyes filled with tears. "And not my friends."

Debbie patted his arm. "It really was a shock. Ray seems fine—a little sore is all."

"How about Eileen?" Harry asked.

"I didn't see her at Good Shepherd," Debbie said. "She was resting."

"How about Gayle?"

Debbie gave him the update.

"I don't know her really, although I do remember her from when she was a girl. She's a few years younger than me."

"Did you know the Jennings family?"

"I was acquainted with them," Harry said. "There was a daughter about Gayle's age, if I remember right."

Debbie nodded. "Yes. Minnie. And Eileen was friends with Minnie's sister-in-law, Marguerite Jennings."

"The woman known as the French war bride?"

"That's right."

"I knew her husband, Bob," Harry said. "He was a carpenter and did repair work on the depot from time to time when I was working as a conductor. He was a good man."

"Did you know Marguerite?"

"No, but of course I knew of her. That said, you hear all sorts of things working around a train depot."

"What did you hear?"

He chuckled. "It sounds ludicrous. I heard she brought some sort of treasure with her from France. That she was from a wealthy family, and they sent it with her." He shook his head. "Of course, people liked to gossip. I think even more back then than now, especially about a newcomer—an outsider. Everyone was curious about her."

"So what do you think?" Debbie asked. "Was there a treasure from her family?"

"Oh, I doubt there was a treasure at all. Someone probably made it up." He shrugged and picked up his cup. "Marguerite passed away a month ago."

"I heard that," Debbie said.

"The sad thing is, I didn't know she was still alive even though we were only living a few blocks from each other. And then, when I heard she passed, I wished I would have had the chance to ask her what it was like to live in Paris through the war and then move to Dennison all those years ago. I wish I'd known her story. The rumor about the treasure was probably the least of it."

Debbie hoped they could still learn more of Marguerite's story, including whether there was some sort of treasure and whether the model depot played a role in safeguarding it.

As Debbie was closing the café just after two, someone knocked on the window. She was ready to point to the closed sign until she saw it was Greg.

She opened the door and swept her arm in front of her. "Come on in. Want some cof—"

He held up the takeout cup in his hands. "I'm good. I was in the neighborhood and decided to stop by instead of texting. How has your day been?"

"Wild." She'd texted him that morning about the accident, and as she finished cleaning up, she gave him an update on Eileen, Ray, and Gayle.

"Jaxon heard Madison was involved in the accident."

"That's right." Debbie hadn't texted that. "I saw her this morning, and she seemed okay."

"Jaxon also heard Dylan was driving."

Debbie nodded.

"Dylan must feel horrible."

Debbie didn't respond.

"His family is new to town," Greg said. "His parents took over the insurance business on Main Street. I stopped by and talked with his dad, Cal, this morning, after Jaxon texted me about the accident."

"What did Cal say?"

"Well, he didn't say anything about the accident, or that Dylan feels terrible. Jaxon heard that at school. Cal just said he's relieved everyone's going to be all right and they're going through the process of sorting through everything."

"Is Jaxon worried about Madison?" Debbie asked.

"I think he was when he first found out, but then he heard she's doing all right. But finding out that Madison was with Dylan completely burst his bubble."

Debbie frowned. He must have still felt hopeful on Friday, even after seeing Madison and Dylan together. "Poor guy."

Greg smiled. "He'll be okay." He took his phone from his pocket and glanced at it. "Want to go to Jaxon's game? I have a few things to see to for the upcoming chamber meeting, but I could swing back by and pick you up. Or meet you there."

"That sounds like fun. I need to run an errand, so I'll meet you there."

"Great." He lifted his cup as if saluting her. "I'll see you soon."

She smiled and waved. "I'm looking forward to it." And she was. She just hoped Jaxon wanted her to come to his football game.

After she finished closing the café and preparing for the next day, Debbie picked up items for Project Fall-iday. Then she headed to the football field at the local park, arriving just as the game started. The day had turned warm, and she slipped out of her jacket as she neared the sidelines. A wave of joy rippled through her. It was a warm fall day with the afternoon sun shining from the blue sky. And she was going to a football game, with a man whose company she was really beginning to enjoy, in the town that she loved. In the moment, she couldn't have been happier.

Debbie kept an eye on Jaxon, playing wide receiver, as she walked to where Greg stood beside another man. When she approached, she realized the second man was Carson. "Hello!" she said as she reached them. "How nice to see you here, Carson. Are you reliving your glory days?"

Carson laughed.

Debbie turned to Greg. "Carson played center way back when. We made it to the finals our senior year."

"Nice," Greg said just as Jaxon caught a pass. "Way to go, Jaxon!" Jaxon was immediately tackled.

"Oh, hey," Greg said, turning to Debbie. "Did Kim find the model depot?"

Debbie shook her head.

At halftime the score was 0-0. Julian ran across the field, carrying his gym bag. He tossed it at Greg's feet, looked up at Debbie, and said, "Hi!" Then he said, "I'll be right back" to his dad. He ran out to the field and tossed a football with another boy until the JV team returned to the field.

Debbie loved how carefree Julian was. She wasn't sure if it was his age, personality, or birth order, but he seemed so much more relaxed than Jaxon.

Halfway through the second half, Jaxon caught another pass at fourth and ten but was immediately tackled again. The ball went to the other team, and they scored with an eighty-yard run on the next play. Then they made the extra kick.

The game ended with a score of 0-7. Greg clapped and yelled, "Shake it off, Mustangs, you'll get 'em next time."

"Good to see the two of you," Carson said. "I'll be in touch, Greg, about our kitchen."

"Looking forward to it," Greg said.

"And I'll see you at the depot." Carson gave Debbie a hug.

"Tell Kristy hello."

He grinned. "I will."

As he walked away, Greg said, "Thank you for passing my name on to Carson."

"Of course," Debbie said. "You're the best."

Greg patted her shoulder and grinned. "I feel the same way about you."

Debbie nudged him with her elbow. "Aw, but I don't redo kitchens. Or entire houses."

"But the way you help people around here has been a huge benefit to our entire community, not to mention the café." His blue eyes twinkled as he spoke. "I'm so glad you moved back to Dennison."

Debbie pressed her lips together for a moment and then said, "Thank you."

Before she could think of what else to say, Jaxon appeared with his bag strapped across his chest. "Can we go home?" He didn't acknowledge Debbie.

Greg crossed his arms. "Anything more you need to say?"

He turned to Debbie but didn't meet her eyes. "Thank you for coming."

"You're welcome. Sorry about the loss. That's rough."

He nodded, still without looking at her, and then turned toward the field. "Julian!" he yelled. "We're leaving!"

Was Jaxon acting that way because his team lost? Or because of the model depot? She desperately wanted him to be innocent—yet he acted so guilty.

"Where are you parked?" Greg asked Debbie.

She motioned toward the street. "Over there."

"We're in the parking lot." He picked up Julian's bag. "Thanks again for coming."

"See you soon." She waved.

"Bye, Debbie!" Julian yelled as he hurried toward them.

That made her smile. As she climbed into her car and fastened her seat belt, she caught sight of Greg walking with Jaxon and Julian toward his truck in the parking lot. Julian ran ahead, and Greg had his arm around Jaxon. It touched her to see father and son together.

And now it was time for her to go to Good Shepherd. She needed to check in on Eileen and Ray.

CHAPTER TEN

$\mathcal{D}$ebbie stared at the visitor log at Good Shepherd, shocked to see Madison's name on the last line. She'd signed in at five fifteen. Why wasn't she at home resting?

After signing in, Debbie headed to the dining hall, which was nearly full. She scanned each table but didn't see Ray, Eileen, or Madison.

As Debbie turned away from the doorway, she nearly bumped into Ashley.

"Oh, hi!" Debbie said.

Ashley smiled. "Any calls about Ray's painting?"

Debbie shook her head. "I'm guessing it hasn't shown up?"

"That's right," Ashley said. "Are you here to see Ray?"

"Eileen," Debbie responded. "And hopefully Ray too."

"They're in the sitting room with Madison. They'll probably head this way for dinner soon."

Debbie wondered if Tony knew Madison was at Good Shepherd, but a voice interrupted her thoughts before she reached the sitting room. "Take a deep breath as you push your shoulders back. Exhale slowly..." When she turned the corner, Debbie stopped. Madison and Eileen were perched on padded folding chairs while Ray sat in his chair. Debbie couldn't see Ray's face, but both Madison and Eileen had their eyes closed.

Madison held her head high.

Eileen leaned back against her chair, her face relaxing as she exhaled.

"I did some research on exercising after a car accident, and we're only going to do breathing exercises today," Madison said. "It'll help with relaxation and getting rid of stiffness. Now we're going to do some deep breathing. First relax your neck and shoulders…"

Debbie stayed put, watching the three for the next few minutes, finding the entire scenario endearing. This was a different side of Madison than what Debbie had seen before. It seemed she was finally getting a glimpse of the girl that both Kim and Eileen adored.

Madison opened her eyes. "That's all for today. I need to get home, but I'll be back Friday at my regular time. Repeat these exercises before you go to bed and then tomorrow, in the morning and at bedtime."

"Thank you, Maddy." Eileen opened her eyes and shifted in her chair, enough to see Debbie. "Well, hello there."

"Hi to all of you," Debbie said.

Ray turned his head, smiling, and winced.

"Are you all right?" Debbie asked.

He rubbed his neck. "Still a little sore. What are you doing here?"

"I came by to check on you and Eileen."

"We're fine." Eileen stood. "Just worried about Gayle."

"How is she? Did Trudy call?"

"Trudy called an hour ago," Ray said. "The surgery was a success, and Gayle is resting." He gestured to Madison. "Thankfully Maddy stopped by and helped us relax a little. It's been a stressful day."

Debbie turned her attention to Madison too. "How are you doing? How's your head?"

Madison sighed. "I'm fine. Dad totally overreacted."

"How's Dylan doing?" Debbie asked.

"I don't know," Madison answered. "I haven't talked to him today." She stood and said, "I'd better get going. See you Friday." She grabbed her sweater from the sofa and headed toward the hall as Ian came around the corner.

Madison stopped and for a moment seemed shocked to see him. Then she said, "Did Dad tell you I was here?"

Ian nodded. "I have a follow-up question for you. We can talk somewhere else if you'd like."

"No, this is fine."

"Do you want some privacy?" Ian asked.

"No. I'd rather they heard, actually." Madison returned to the sofa, and Eileen sat down beside her.

Debbie hesitated a moment. She was glad Tony knew where Madison was. He must have changed his mind about her going to Good Shepherd.

Eileen took Madison's hand. "Sweetie, what's going on?"

Madison exhaled, rather loudly, inflating her cheeks as she did. "I know I'm suspected of taking the model depot and Ray's painting, and it doesn't help that I was with Dylan last night when he hit you all."

Debbie sat down. Dylan claimed that Gayle sped across the tracks, but Madison said it was his fault.

"I didn't take the model depot. I didn't take the painting," she said. "And I want to do whatever I need to do to prove I'm innocent. I was acting weird the night the depot disappeared, but that doesn't mean I took it. And I'd never take something out of a resident's room. Leading the exercise class here is my favorite thing. I wouldn't jeopardize it—not for anything."

"All right," Ian said. "I appreciate you being open about all of this."

"So what do I have to do to prove I'm innocent?" she asked. "Let someone search my room? Take a lie detector test? What should I do?"

"Well, lie detector tests are expensive, and we don't use them for minor offenses." Ian clasped his hands together and leaned forward. "At this point, the best way to prove your innocence is for us to find out what happened to both the model depot and the painting. If there's a thief, we need to find out who it is." Ian looked from Madison to Debbie. "The more we work together, the better our chances of finding the depot and the painting."

"Cool." Madison pushed up the sleeves of her sweater. "I'm all in. What do I do to help figure out what happened?"

"Well, we keep asking questions. And keep looking for both items."

"What about suspects?" Madison said. "There's me. And Jaxon and maybe Julian. Anyone else?"

Ian shook his head. "Actually, there aren't any suspects, officially. This isn't a criminal investigation."

"But it's hurting my reputation," Madison said.

Debbie put her hands on her knees. "What, exactly, is going on to hurt your reputation?"

"The kids at school are saying I'm a thief. That I was mad Dad wouldn't let me go to homecoming with Dylan, so I stole the depot." Madison wiped her eyes. "And other kids are saying it was Jaxon. I feel bad about that. Some are even saying Dylan took it."

"Do you think either one of them is guilty?" Debbie asked.

"Absolutely not," Madison answered. "I feel bad their reputations are being questioned too."

"Well, reputations aren't as important as character," Ian said. "Keep your head about you, and let's keep trying to sort this out."

A few minutes later, in the parking lot, Ian said, "Debbie, I have a favor to ask."

"Really?" She couldn't remember Ian ever asking her for anything, except coffee or a pastry. "What's that?"

He held up his phone. "I have an interview I need to do back at the station. I told Janet I'd be home for dinner—she fixed tacos—but I'm going to be late. Really late. Would you go eat with her?"

Debbie threw her arms up in the air. "Oh, the sacrifices I make for you." She patted him on the back. "Of course. But don't expect us to save you any," she teased.

He laughed. "I'll get something from the vending machine, but first I'll text Janet."

Debbie waited till he was done texting and then said, "Actually, I'm really happy to. I wasn't looking forward to going home alone."

Ian glanced up from his phone. "Any specific reason?"

Debbie shrugged. "Probably more than one."

Ian smiled. "Is Greg busy tonight?"

Debbie raised her eyebrows. "Who said anything about Greg?"

Ian laughed. "I imagine he's busy every night. Football practices. Back-to-school nights. Chamber meetings." Ian put his phone in his jacket pocket. "I don't know how he does it."

"Neither do I," Debbie said. She paused. "You never asked Madison your follow-up question."

He smiled. "I didn't, did I? I just wanted to see her reaction to me showing up unannounced."

"And what did you think about her reaction?"

"Either she's innocent, or she's a really good actor."

Fifteen minutes later, Debbie and Janet dished up their carnitas tacos in the Shaw family kitchen. "Thank you for coming over," Janet said. "I know Ian feels horrible for not making it home for dinner—and he should." Janet chuckled but then her voice grew serious. "It's so quiet with Tiffany gone. I didn't realize how much she filled our house, especially during a week like this with Ian working so much."

Debbie sprinkled chopped onions and then cilantro on top of her carnitas spread across the warm tortilla. "Well, I'm sorry Ian has been working so much, but I'm happy to fill in." She dished corn salad onto her plate. "You know I miss Tiffany too. I move back to town and then"—she snapped her fingers—"she's gone."

"That's how I feel," Janet said. "Not the part about moving back to town, but I can't comprehend how it all went so quickly. I mean, everyone told me it would, but I didn't believe it because some of those years did kind of drag." She grinned. "But then suddenly I realized it did go that fast, and it's over."

Debbie put her arm around Janet and pulled her close. "At least you have me."

Janet laughed again. "God works in mysterious ways."

"That's for sure." Debbie grabbed the glass of lemonade Janet had poured for her and headed to the breakfast nook that looked over the now-dark backyard.

After saying the blessing, Janet asked Debbie how Greg and his boys were. Debbie told her about Jaxon not looking her in the eye after the football game.

"Don't read anything into it. He's fourteen," Janet said.

"True." Debbie took a bite of her taco. "This is delicious."

"Thank you. We used to have Taco Tuesdays when Tiffany was younger. I have an entire collection of recipes."

"It's Wednesday," Debbie said.

Janet laughed. "See, I'm all discombobulated."

Debbie took another bite. "You should write a cookbook."

Janet rubbed her palms together. "Mom and I were talking about that the other day. With her experience, with her help, I'm thinking I might give it a try." Janet's mother had just retired after a long career in publishing.

"That's awesome." Debbie set her taco on her plate. "Tacos? Pastries? Cakes?"

"I'm thinking about an 'everything-homecooked cookbook' with a few recipes from each category."

Debbie smiled. "I'd buy it."

"Great." Janet grinned. "So would my mom."

"And my mom," Debbie said.

"That's three."

"And we could sell copies in the café."

"Oh," Janet said, "I hadn't thought of that."

"You could name it *Recipes from Dennison*. And add a few historical recipes, including the—"

"—doughnut recipe!" Janet slapped the tabletop. "What a great idea!"

Just the thought of a cookbook project warmed Debbie. Janet deserved more recognition for her cooking, and it would be great marketing for the café too.

"Speaking of projects," Janet said, "any new discoveries about the depot or Ray's painting?"

Debbie shook her head.

"How is Madison?"

Debbie told Janet about stumbling on Madison leading Ray and Eileen in breathing exercises. "It was really heartwarming. Then Ian stopped by to supposedly ask her a follow-up question, but it was a ruse to see how she'd react to seeing him again."

Janet shook her head. "He has all sorts of tricks like that." She took another bite. "Any other leads?"

Suddenly a picture of Kristy on homecoming night at the station popped into Debbie's mind. Kristy had been carrying a large bag...

"Well." Debbie set her taco on her plate. "I wonder about Kristy."

"Why?"

"She was in the museum that night with a bag big enough to stash half the model train layout in, so the depot would have fit just fine. And remember how sneaky she got our last couple of years of high school."

"I remember her being out of sorts, but I don't remember her being sneaky."

"She took my favorite earrings. The gold hoops from you."

"What are you talking about?"

"You don't remember?"

Janet shook her head. "No."

"The three of us were at my house after school on my birthday our junior year. I took my earrings off—you had just given them to me at school—and put them on my desk. After everyone left, my earrings were gone."

"And you've blamed Kristy all these years?"

"Well, I knew you didn't take them."

Janet shook her head. "I can't believe you're still thinking about that all these years later."

Debbie crossed her arms. "And then Kristy got so weird after that."

"Did you accuse her of taking your earrings?"

Debbie's face grew warm. "I asked her about them."

"Maybe that's why she got weird." Janet wrapped her hand around her glass. "You know, I've thought about Kristy and those last two years of high school. Did you know her mom was sick?"

"My mom thought maybe she was—did you know?"

"I didn't know at the time, but I remember her mother lost a lot of weight and she was gone some. Maybe she had to go out of town to a hospital or something."

"Why didn't Kristy tell us?"

Janet shrugged. "People have their reasons. Maybe it's what her mom wanted."

Debbie had a sinking feeling. Had she been so obtuse in high school? She saw herself as empathetic and caring, but she'd been a teenager. Just as Madison and Jaxon were now, except she'd been a little older. She would pray about this later, but for now she changed the subject. "I haven't made any progress with figuring out what happened to Ray's painting. I can't help but wonder if it was taken because the thief thought it might be connected to the rumored gold coins that Marguerite brought from France."

"Can I see the painting again?" Janet asked.

Debbie took her phone out of her pocket, pulled up the photo, and handed her phone to Janet. "Here it is."

Janet zoomed in on the painting. Then she asked, "How about if I do some research tomorrow and see what I can find out about artists in Dennison through the years? Maybe I can find out who painted this. The more angles we explore the better, right?"

"Right," Debbie replied. "We have the French war bride connection, the artist connection, the depot connection, the gold coins… We need to figure out what the possible motivations for stealing the depot and the painting could be." She paused and then added, "But I still think, despite my holding a grudge for twenty-six years, that Kristy could be a suspect."

Janet rolled her eyes. "I don't think so. Let's see what I can find out about local artists. If Marguerite painted Ray's picture and left clues in it, we need to find out what the clues mean. And who knows about them." She held up her glass of lemonade. "That makes more sense than accusing someone because of something you *think* they did over two and a half decades ago."

Debbie held up her glass too, but she wasn't convinced. "I hope your research helps crack this case wide open."

Janet clinked her glass against Debbie's. "Oh, I can almost guarantee you that it will."

Debbie loved Janet's confidence. Especially when it came to writing a cookbook. As far as cracking the possible code in the painting? She wasn't as sure about that.

CHAPTER ELEVEN

*A*fter the morning rush ended, Janet washed her hands and took off her apron. "I'm heading to the library to go through the *Evening Chronicle* for a couple of hours. Everything's prepped for lunch. I'll be back before noon."

"Perfect," Debbie said. "Thank you."

A few minutes later, as Paulette took the order of a mom and her preschool daughter, Kim came into the café. "Hi, Debbie. Can I get a cup of coffee to go?"

Debbie poured the coffee and handed it to Kim. "Running late?"

"Yes. I was over at Tony and Madison's this morning." Kim took a sip of the coffee. "She asked me to search her room and the house in general for the depot."

"Interesting. Was Ian involved in the search?"

Kim shook her head. "I didn't see any need to involve him. Madison's so desperate to prove that she didn't take the depot or Ray's painting that she begged me to come search everything." Kim stood. "She's really tidy, so it didn't take long. And the entire house is just over twelve hundred square feet, so that didn't take long either, but then Tony and I had a long chat. The car accident really scared him—and the fact that Madison slipped out of the house without him knowing it. He thought she was doing homework in her room."

Debbie remembered sneaking out a few times in high school. Sometimes to ride around with older kids. One time to meet Janet by the railroad tracks to talk through something they thought couldn't wait. She never slipped out to meet a boy though. She also never got caught. Did her parents know? She'd have to ask Mom sometime.

"Tony's afraid he's not doing a good job and that maybe she'd be better off with her mom."

Debbie frowned. "What do you think?"

"Well, selfishly, we want her here. Mom, Tony, Neal, and me. But I don't know, maybe she should be with her mother."

Debbie thought of Greg, Jaxon, and Julian. Being a single parent was hard, and Greg didn't have a choice. His wife died. But he seemed to be doing just fine. And, from what she could tell, Tony was a loving and caring father too. If Madison wanted to live with him in Dennison, she hoped they could make it work.

"I'd better get going," Kim said. "See you later."

"See you," Debbie replied. She turned to the display case. Just because Kim didn't find the model depot or painting in Madison's room didn't mean she didn't take one of them—or both. Or that Jaxon didn't take the depot and give it to her. Perhaps Jaxon took the depot and Madison took the painting. Or maybe Dylan took both. Perhaps Madison regretted her part in it now, like Ian said often happens. Hopefully, if that was the case, she'd return both soon.

Debbie put an apple fritter and a chocolate muffin on plates for the mother and daughter and then on a tray while Paulette made a pumpkin spice latte and a hot chocolate.

After that, no customers came in, and Debbie worked on the details for the fall train rides at the corner table while Paulette refilled coffee cups and wiped tables.

As Debbie jotted down a to-do list in her notebook, her thoughts drifted to Janet researching artists in Dennison. Debbie remembered a local artist visiting her class in the fifth grade, but he was a middle-aged man who made sculptures of comic book heroes. It was fascinating but about as different from what Marguerite did as possible.

It wasn't as if there was an art gallery in Dennison or anything like that either. She hoped Janet could find something.

The lunch rush started at eleven thirty. By noon Paulette and Debbie were swamped and Janet still hadn't come back. Finally, at twelve twenty, she hurried into the café. "Sorry," she whispered as she passed by Debbie in the kitchen to wash her hands.

When she returned, she said, "I'll take over. Go ahead and help Paulette."

Debbie delivered soup, sandwiches, salads, and bowls of pasta for the next half hour, while Paulette took more orders. A half hour after that, the flow of customers finally slowed.

Debbie stepped into the kitchen. "So did you learn anything about artists in town? And about Marguerite in particular?"

"Yes and yes." Janet nodded. "Be patient. I'll tell you after we have everything under control."

Paulette left, and Debbie cleared more tables, loaded the dishwasher, made a few beverages for to-go orders, and finally turned the sign to Closed. Then she made pumpkin spice lattes for herself and Janet.

"Time for a break," she called to Janet. "Everyone's gone. Can you come out and sit for a few minutes before you leave?"

Janet called from the kitchen, "I'll be right there, after I dish up two bowls of soup for us."

Debbie set the lattes on the table closest to the kitchen door, and a minute later, Janet joined her. The soup was tortellini with sausage and kale, and it was delicious.

Debbie took a bite and swallowed. "So what did you find?"

"First, I looked for a 1944 Dennison High School yearbook, thinking I'd figure out who Anna was—but they didn't have that year."

"Bummer."

"Yes. Sadly, they're missing quite a few years." Janet picked up her fork. "As far as Marguerite's art career, she only had one show in the area. At the Claymont Library—her flower paintings in 1962. She did offer art lessons during the late '60s and early '70s. There are several ads in the paper for that and one feature story. She taught elementary children after school in her home studio. Judging from the photograph, they were all girls. Unfortunately, none of the articles included anything about the model depot or the other paintings, although there was a quote from Marguerite saying that she had a painting stolen from her portfolio on the night the exhibit opened."

"That's odd. Why would anyone steal one of her paintings?"

Janet shrugged and then took a bite while Debbie waited in anticipation.

"Did you find anything in the articles that might help?"

"No."

Debbie rolled her eyes.

Janet smiled. "But I did find some other interesting things."

Debbie leaned forward.

"A volunteer at the library did genealogical searches through a couple of their databases, just to see what she could find. Sofia's US birth certificate popped up. It was issued on April 3, 1947. She wasn't quite two at the time. Her birth date was July 7, 1945."

"Wasn't she born in France?"

"Yes. The US birth certificate lists her as foreign born. I assumed they had to get a US birth certificate when she arrived in the US—she would have had citizenship since Bob Jennings was her father. But the volunteer—her name is Esther Wilcox—said it appeared to be a birth certificate from an adoption."

"An adoption? Marguerite and Bob adopted Sofia?"

Janet lowered her voice. "I have no idea."

"Why did the volunteer say that?"

"She said it looked like other adoption birth certificates she'd seen before."

"Maybe that's because it was a new birth certificate. It doesn't mean she was adopted."

"Could be." Janet took a sip of her latte and then said, "I found one other interesting tidbit."

"What's that?"

"It was in a newspaper article from August 1948." Janet cradled her mug in her hands. "Marguerite won a blue ribbon at the county fair for a drawing of the Dennison Depot."

Debbie perked up. "Was there a photo of the drawing?"

Janet shook her head. "Not even a description. But it seemed Marguerite had an interest in the depot long before Bob made the model and she painted it."

After Janet left, Debbie finished cleaning the café, prepped for the next day, and then headed down to the museum to speak with Kim. She explained what Janet had been told about the birth certificate.

"I don't think the woman at the library knew what she was talking about," Kim said. "But I think you should stop by Sofia's and tell her what she said. I'm sure Sofia has a copy of her birth certificate. She can probably just look at it herself. I'll call and tell her you're on your way."

"Tell her I'm walking, so it will be ten minutes or so," Debbie said. A couple of minutes later, she stepped out of the depot into the bright October sunshine and brisk afternoon. She took a deep breath, inhaling the faint scent of woodsmoke. Someone was enjoying an afternoon fire.

As she passed Harry's house, Crosby came down the steps from the porch. Debbie stopped and clapped her hands. Then she met him halfway up the sidewalk and rubbed his ears. When she finished, she pointed to the porch. "Go!"

Crosby wagged his tail, turned around, and trotted back up the steps, and Debbie continued toward Sofia's house. When she arrived, she stepped onto the porch and Sofia swung the front door open.

"Debbie," she said. "I'm so happy to see you. Kim said you had a look at my birth certificate."

"My friend Janet did, with some help from a volunteer at the library."

Sofia motioned for Debbie to step inside. "I can assure you I'm not adopted. I have my birth certificate out, along with Dad's." She led the way to the table in the dining room. "Yes, the issue date is 1947, but it shows I was born July 7, 1945. Under normal circumstances, I think they would have been able to get a US birth certificate from the embassy in Paris, but because of the war, maybe they couldn't." She picked up the birth certificate and showed it to Debbie.

It was just as Janet said. It read *Foreign Born*, and gave the date of birth and the date the birth certificate was filed.

"I'm not an expert on any of this," Debbie said. "But I don't see any indication of an adoption."

"I guess I'll know for sure soon," Sofia said. "I sent in a DNA test a few weeks ago to try to connect with family in France. Mother was never very forthcoming about her parents, let alone other relatives."

"I wouldn't worry about it," Debbie said. "Janet was looking at information about artists in Dennison, including your mother, to try to find out anything she could about Ray's painting. We're hoping exploring different angles might open up a lead to finding the depot. The library volunteer did a search on your mother and somehow came up with your birth certificate." Debbie grimaced. "I hope you don't mind. It sounded innocent enough when Janet told me, but now it sounds a little intrusive."

"It reminds me of all those questions about Mama when I was little, those suspicions," Sofia said.

"I'm sorry," Debbie said. "I didn't mean to upset you. I'm sure it's nothing."

Sofia sighed. "I hope so. But I don't mind Janet researching our family if it helps figure out if there really is a collection of gold coins, and where it is."

Debbie handed the birth certificate back to Sofia. "Have you found any other information that might be helpful?"

"No." Sofia put her birth certificate on top of her father's. "Speaking of certificates, I was hoping to find Mama and Daddy's marriage certificate and my original French birth certificate, but neither of those have turned up either. I'm hoping they're all in the same place. I know things were chaotic during and after the war in France, but they would have needed at least a marriage certificate to get Mama and me on the ship."

Debbie nodded in agreement. "I hope you find them."

Sofia sighed and gestured toward the birth certificates. "I'm sure the woman at the library was just being helpful. I never told my parents this—it would have broken Mama's heart and made Daddy angry—but throughout my school years I had a few kids tell me I didn't belong here, that I should go back to France and take my mother with me. That my daddy wasn't really my daddy."

Debbie stepped toward Sofia. "Can I give you a hug?"

"Please," she answered.

Debbie gave her a long hug. "You belonged here as a child, and you belong here now. And you'd belong here even if your father had adopted you. Obviously, he loved you very much."

"He did." Sofia smiled. "Merci."

CHAPTER TWELVE

Debbie didn't get a chance to call Ray because, just as she reached her house, he called her. She answered the call quickly as she hurried up her stairs. "Hello, Ray."

"Debbie? Is that you?"

"It's me. How are you? How is Gayle?"

"Hold on a minute." He paused. "I needed to change the phone to my other ear."

"How are you?" Debbie asked again. "How is Gayle?"

"That's why I'm calling. She's doing all right. I hate to ask this, but could you give me a ride up to see her?"

"I'd love to." Debbie started back down her porch steps and toward her car. "I'm on my way."

A half hour later Debbie rolled Ray into Gayle's hospital room.

The bed was in a near-upright position, and Gayle smiled at them. Her short white hair looked as if it had been recently washed, and her dimples punctuated her face.

"Sit down," Gayle said. "Trudy went to get some dinner, finally. I have bad news and good news."

Debbie pulled a chair closer to the bed and then wheeled Ray as close as she could to Gayle.

Ray leaned forward. "The bad news first, of course."

"My Lincoln is totaled."

"I'm so sorry," Debbie and Ray said in unison.

"Thank you," Gayle said. "I'm afraid it means my independence is totaled too. I may have to figure out how to use those rideshare apps." She sighed. "I really can't imagine getting another car now, but I'll have to see how I feel in a week or two."

"What's the good news?" Ray asked.

"If I get out tomorrow, Trudy is going to take me home."

"So soon?" Ray leaned back in his chair. By the sadness in his voice, he didn't see it as good news. "I hoped I'd be able to see you for a few more days."

Her eyes twinkled. "Maybe they won't release me tomorrow." She held up her casted wrist. "Maybe they'll make me stay longer."

"Well," Ray said, "we don't want that. I just thought maybe you could get out and Trudy would stay here with you."

Gayle reached out her good arm toward him, and he took her hand in his. "I'd like that. I really would."

After a moment of silence, Debbie slipped out of her jacket. "How's your concussion?"

"Much better," Gayle said. "The headaches have nearly stopped, but I still have a no-screens rule in place." She grinned. "But visitors are fine."

After some general conversation, Gayle said, "I've been thinking more about Minnie Jennings and Bob, Marguerite, and Sofia. And about Anna, although I still haven't remembered her last name. Minnie and I were so taken with Anna, with her being older and all. We were twelve when she graduated from high school. Her father worked for the railroad. They lived several blocks away. After she graduated, Anna worked at the canteen, serving doughnuts to the troops going through. She had auburn hair, deep brown eyes, and always wore bright red lipstick. Her family moved here from Chicago, and she seemed far more mature than most of the girls around."

Ray let go of Gayle's hand. "Anna doesn't sound like she was Bob's type."

"Exactly," Gayle said.

"Was Marguerite Bob's type?" Debbie asked.

Gayle smiled. "In an odd way, yes. Marguerite was genuine, where Anna put a lot of work into being seen as sophisticated. Bob was easygoing, dependable, and never wanted anything more than to stay in Dennison and raise a family."

Gayle adjusted her pillows, closed her eyes, and continued. "Minnie liked the idea of Bob leaving behind a sweetheart, but I'm not sure Bob ever thought of Anna as anyone more than to go on a couple of casual dates or exchange a few letters with. So much letter writing went on back then." She opened her eyes and turned to Ray again. "Remember? Dad, Mom, and I wrote to you every couple of days. Minnie wrote to you. I wrote to Bob."

"I remember," he said. "Those letters meant the world to us. I don't know how we would have gotten through the war without them."

A lump formed in Debbie's throat as Ray reminisced. It was hard to imagine a world where one couldn't text and call, where one relied entirely on letters that took weeks to get to their destination.

Gayle picked up her story again. "Anyway, Anna resented that Bob 'dumped' her without writing to tell her about Marguerite, but

Bob also wrote Minnie and his parents less frequently by the summer of 1944 and then through most of '45. He worked as a clerk for a colonel and moved around a lot, from Caen to Paris and then farther east, and then back to Paris. He said a lot of his letters didn't get through. I think Anna's pride was hurt."

"Did she still live in town when Bob came home?" Debbie asked. "And then when Marguerite and Sofia arrived?"

"Yes. I don't remember all the details, but she was a little dramatic when Bob returned. Minnie said Anna confronted him on their front porch. By the time Marguerite arrived, I think Anna had spread gossip about her in town. After that, Anna moved to Chicago for a few years, but then she came back to town again."

"Really? Why?" Debbie asked.

"I'm not sure," Gayle said. "I was off to college by then. But probably to get married. I think she'd finally given up on Bob Jennings."

After Debbie took Ray back to Good Shepherd, she headed south to Sunny's Apple Orchard to buy the cider for the upcoming events. It was 5:42, and they closed at six. When she arrived, vehicles filled the parking lot, including Greg's.

She parked beside it and then headed to the store. When she went inside, she didn't see Greg, but she did see about ten boys who all appeared to be middle-school age. She searched the group for Julian, but he saw her first.

"Debbie!" he called out from near a shelf of honey.

She waved. "What are you doing here?"

"My football team is having dinner here." He nudged the boy next to him. "Sunny is Monty's grandma. She owns this place."

Monty. As in Monty and Brent. And Roger.

"That sounds like fun," Debbie said. "What's on the menu?"

"Hot dogs and hamburgers," Monty answered. "We're barbecuing in Granny's backyard."

That sounded perfect for a fall evening.

"What are you doing here?" Julian asked.

"Picking up cider for the Fall-iday events on Saturday."

Julian's eyes grew wide. "That sounds like fun too. Will there be doughnuts?"

Debbie laughed. "Yes, at the depot. And pumpkin sugar cookies on the train."

Julian rubbed his hands together. "I'm going to ask Dad if we can go."

"Speaking of, I saw his truck in the parking lot."

"He's here, barbecuing in the backyard."

"Fun," Debbie said. "Tell him I said hello." She waved and said, "See you soon."

She headed toward the counter as Monty asked, "Who's that?"

"A friend of ours," Julian said, heading toward the door. "She's the new owner of the Whistle Stop Café."

Debbie's heart warmed as she approached the counter. A woman with long dark hair asked, "May I help you?"

"I'm Debbie Albright, co-owner of the Whistlestop Café." She loved saying that. "I'm here to pick up an order of apple cider."

"Oh." The woman closed the cash register drawer. "I'll check the storeroom."

Debbie watched the boys leave the shop, laughing and poking at each other as they went.

The clerk came back. "I don't see anything in there. I'll call Sunny and see where it is." She pulled a phone from her apron pocket and placed the call. Debbie stepped over to the shelf of local honey for sale.

When the woman ended the call she said, "Sunny said she'll get the cider from the warehouse. She'll send someone right over with it."

"Isn't she busy with the barbecue?"

"It's not a problem." The clerk extended her hand. "I'm Amanda Dunn, Sunny's daughter-in-law, Roger's wife, and Monty's mom. I saw you talking with Julian."

Roger. The man out in the parking lot the night the depot was taken. Debbie shook Amanda's hand. She didn't look old enough to be Monty's mother. "I'm pleased to meet you."

"Roger loves that old depot. In fact, he still has his model train set from when he was little because he loves the place so much."

"Interesting," Debbie said. Exactly how much did Roger love the depot?

"I've seen you at Julian's games with Greg," Amanda said. "At Jaxon's too. Our older son plays on his team."

"How nice," Debbie said.

"Greg's a great guy."

"He is," Debbie said. Besides wondering how much Roger loved the depot, Debbie was also trying to figure out just how young Amanda might be.

"Did you grow up here?"

She shook her head. "I used to live in Columbus. I met Roger, Monty's dad, at a trade show there. I worked for the state agricultural department."

"How long have you lived in Dennison?" Debbie asked.

"Three years now." She smiled. "I'm the boys' stepmom, but their mom isn't in their lives much, so they asked me to refer to myself as their mother."

"Got it." Debbie glanced toward the door. The shop was empty, and the door was closed. "So how is it, being a stepmom to boys?"

At least ten different emotions passed across Amanda's face. Then she laughed. "It depends on the day, but I can say this much—it's definitely worth it."

The door opened, and Debbie turned toward it.

"Hello, ma'am. Sunny sent me. I have your order." Greg, the sleeves of his flannel shirt rolled up to his elbows, stood in the doorway with two boxes stacked on a dolly. "Where are you parked?"

Debbie grinned. "Right next to you." She turned and waved to Amanda. "It's been so nice to meet you. I'll look for you at the next game."

"I'll look for you too," Amanda said. Then she took a step away from the counter. "See you at the barbecue, Greg!"

"I'll be back there in a flash. I don't want Roger to burn the burgers."

Amanda laughed. "I'll check on them if I get there first."

As they walked toward her car, Debbie said, "How did you get roped into carting my cider?"

Greg steered the dolly to the right and then to the left as he answered. "Believe it or not, I volunteered when I overheard Sunny on the phone."

"Well, thank you," she said. "I appreciate it." When she reached her car, she raised the back, and Greg lifted one of the boxes in and then the other. "Want to join us for the barbecue?"

Debbie hesitated. "I think I'd be intruding."

"Julian would be fine with it."

She didn't doubt that. He would probably barely notice. "Thank you," she said. "But not tonight."

He looked like a sad puppy for a minute. "Is it okay if I ask you to join us for a future event?"

"Yes," she said. "I'd like that very much."

She walked around to the driver's door but then turned and watched Greg walk toward the fenced backyard. He zigzagged along as he pushed the dolly, his step light and quick. Was he whistling? She listened carefully. It sounded as if he was whistling. She loved how carefree he seemed when he lived a fast-paced life between his contractor business, his work for the chamber, and all the running around he did as a single dad. He was calm, collected, and steadfast.

She climbed into the car. Maybe she should have stayed for the barbecue. What had stopped her? She gripped the steering wheel. Amanda noticing her at Julian's and Jaxon's games had unnerved her. She hadn't thought much about others watching her and Greg and speculating. But of course they would. Greg was a beloved member of the community, and a single dad.

She knew moving back to Dennison and buying the café would put her under the small-town magnifying glass. She just hadn't thought what it would be like to be under there with someone else.

The next morning, after the breakfast rush, Debbie and Janet started a production line to make the pumpkin sugar cookies for the Fall-iday train rides. As Debbie rolled out the dough that Janet had made earlier that morning, she felt a little overwhelmed with everything they needed to get done. But then her mom stepped into the kitchen.

Debbie raised the rolling pin in midair.

Mom grinned. "Need some help?"

Janet extended both hands in a big-hearted gesture. "Yes, absolutely, Becca!"

Debbie lowered the rolling pin back down to the dough. "How did you know we needed help?"

"I knew you'd be making something for the events tomorrow, on top of all of your usual daily tasks." She motioned toward the sink. "I'll wash up and you can put me to work."

Debbie kept rolling, Janet kept cutting, and Mom set the cookies on the cookie sheets and then popped them into the oven.

After a few minutes, Mom said, "We need to talk about your birthday."

Debbie froze. She had totally forgotten and hadn't talked with Mom about Kristy's proposal.

"Yeah, we do need to talk about your birthday," Janet said. "Did you tell Kristy yes?"

"Kristy? What does she have to do with your birthday?" Mom asked.

"She offered to host a birthday dinner for me," Debbie said. "I've been meaning to talk to you. Carson will cook—it turns out he's quite the chef. And Kristy will decorate—"

"And I'll bake the cake," Janet interjected.

"Perfect." Mom clapped her hands. "Are Dad and I invited?"

"Of course you're invited," Debbie said. "I just keep forgetting to talk with you about it. Do you mind it not being at your house?"

Mom put another cookie on the tray. "Of course not. I think it would be a lot of fun to have dinner at Kristy and Carson's."

"Great," Debbie said, but she felt a little unsettled. What if they discovered before the birthday dinner that Kristy had taken the model depot? She finished rolling out the last of the cookie dough and said, "I'll text Kristy. And then help Paulette take orders. We have several full tables."

"I'll get ready to start cooking," Janet said.

Debbie sent Kristy the text and then busied herself taking orders and making drinks. Each time she stepped into the kitchen, Mom was at the back counter, sliding baked cookies off the cookie sheets, humming as she worked.

Paulette left at one, and soon after, Mom declared that she'd finished baking the cookies.

"How about a sandwich and a bowl of soup?" Debbie asked. "I don't know what we would have done without you."

"I'll take a cup of soup and half a sandwich," Mom said.

"Perfect. We can split the sandwich." Debbie turned to Janet. "Do you want one too?"

Janet nodded. "I'll make them while you clear the tables."

When Debbie was clearing the last table, her phone dinged. Kristy. WONDERFUL! LET'S PLAN ON 6:30. WE'LL INVITE JANET AND IAN, YOUR PARENTS, KIM FROM THE MUSEUM, AND YOUR FRIEND GREG. THAT WILL MAKE NINE OF US—THE PERFECT DINNER PARTY. I'LL MAKE SURE EVERYONE KNOWS.

Debbie texted back, THANK YOU SO MUCH! I'M REALLY LOOKING FORWARD TO IT.

As Debbie slipped her phone into her apron pocket, Carson came into the café.

"How's the birthday girl?" he asked.

"Hey," Debbie said. "I have another week of being forty-three."

He laughed. "Counting the days before turning a year older? I think we're all at that stage in life."

Debbie actually didn't mind turning a year older. The alternative would be much worse. "What can I get you?"

"A cup of coffee to go," Carson said. "I have a Monday morning deadline. I need to get a lot of work done this afternoon—and over the weekend."

"What's your deadline for?" Debbie asked as she poured the coffee.

"I'm working on an article for a history publication about Dennison and the railroad during World War II. I had a few last-minute questions for Kim." Carson picked up the cup of coffee that Debbie placed before him. "The eightieth anniversary of the end of World War II is coming up in a couple of years. I've pitched a book idea about the railroad system on the home front to a publishing house. Getting articles published first might help me get a contract."

"Nice," Debbie said. "Both you and Kristy have such interesting and successful careers."

Carson smiled, leaned forward, and lowered his voice. "Kristy is far more successful than I am. She's so modest she'd never disclose this, but she's a big deal in the gaming-design world."

"Really?"

He took a sip of his coffee and then said, "Let's just say she contributes far more to our household than I do."

Debbie started wiping down the counter and said, "But you cook dinner. So it's a win-win situation, right? I know it would be for me."

He laughed. "I just had a text from Kristy a few minutes ago. She said we're hosting your birthday dinner."

"Yes," Debbie said. "It's so kind of the two of you. I really appreciate it."

"We're happy to do it." Carson took another sip of his coffee and then said, "It means so much to Kristy. She wanted to move back to Dennison but was hesitant."

"Why?" Debbie asked.

"She has some bad memories…"

Debbie stopped wiping and waited.

"Her mom had cancer our last two years of high school. I had no idea. I hardly knew Kristy then. But that was a hard time for her."

Debbie felt a pang of guilt. "What happened to her mother?"

"She passed away our senior year of college. Her parents had moved to Columbus, mostly so her mother was closer to better medical care. Kristy and I started dating around the time her mother died."

"Oh, that's so sad."

Carson nodded. "I guess her mother was super secretive, and people in town didn't know she had cancer."

Debbie thought of Mom suspecting something was going on with Kristy's mother. She'd been right.

"Anyway," Carson said, "we're glad we're here. And the warmth you and Janet have shown Kristy has made the transition much easier."

"I'm so glad it has." Debbie's phone buzzed in her pocket. "It's wonderful to have both of you back in Dennison."

Just then Mom came out of the kitchen. "I thought I heard your voice, Carson. How are you? How is Kristy doing?"

As Carson answered, Debbie checked her phone. It was Greg. WANT TO GO TO THE VARSITY FOOTBALL GAME TONIGHT? I'M TAKING THE BOYS.

She had the event the next day and would need to get up early and work with Janet to get everything ready. On the other hand, she had told Greg just the day before to invite her again.

SURE, she texted back. WHAT TIME?

GAME STARTS AT 7. HOW ABOUT DINNER AT 5 AT MY PLACE? WE'RE GRILLING PIZZAS. AMANDA AND ROGER AND THEIR BOYS ARE COMING TOO.

She hesitated a moment. Was this how it started when one was interested in a family man? She and Greg hadn't even gone on a date. On the other hand, dinner at his house with another family sounded like fun. Hopefully Jaxon would be okay with her being there.

"Debbie?"

She turned to her mother, who said, "I was asking about the model depot. Kim hasn't found it yet?"

Debbie shook her head as she slipped her phone back into her pocket. She'd answer Greg later.

CHAPTER THIRTEEN

*S*he arrived at Greg's house at 4:58 with a pan of gooey brownies that she'd managed to bake after she closed the café. The late afternoon was still warm. Hammer, the family dog, barked a greeting as she opened the back gate. "Hi, boy," she said. "Wait until I put these down."

"Hello!" Greg called out and then came and took the brownies. "Thank you for bringing these."

"You're welcome." Debbie bent down and petted Hammer. Greg had insisted he didn't need her to contribute anything, but then she insisted she wanted to. She'd won.

She glanced around the backyard as Greg put the food on a folding table. The Dunns hadn't arrived yet, and the boys were nowhere to be seen. Even though sunset was an hour and a half away, Greg had lit a few torches and turned on an Ohio State neon sign too.

Besides the food table, there was a table with an umbrella and an area with seating and a firepit.

"It's lovely back here," Debbie said.

"Thank you." Greg gestured toward the empty flower bed. "I'm not so great with the gardening, but the barbecuing usually works out all right."

"Well, we all have to prioritize," Debbie said.

He grinned. "The Dunns are running a few minutes late." He stepped to the grill. "I'm precooking the pizza crusts. Then we'll put sauce and toppings on them, and I'll cook them the rest of the way."

"Fun." Debbie hadn't had barbecued pizzas before. Greg had containers of sauce, cheese, pepperoni, mushrooms, olives, and other toppings on the table.

Julian came bounding out the back door. "Hi, Debbie!"

Before she could answer him, he called out, "Dad, the Dunns just pulled up." Then he ran out the gate, leaving it open.

Amanda came through the gate, carrying a veggie platter. "Debbie, it's nice to see you again so soon!" She nodded to the man following her. "This is Roger. Roger, Debbie."

As they both said, "Nice to meet you," Julian, Monty, and another boy came running through the gate, passing a football back and forth.

"You met Monty," Amanda said. "The older one is Brent."

"Hello, Brent," Debbie called out. "I'm Debbie."

Brent stopped, the football in his hands. "Nice to meet you." He turned to Greg. "Where's Jaxon?"

"He got to suit up for the game tonight." Greg grinned. "He found out this afternoon."

"Wow." Brent's eyes lit up. "That's really cool." He passed the ball over the grill to Julian, who was standing in the yard, waving his arms. The ball sailed through the air—and straight through his hands.

Julian fell to the ground as he moaned, "I can't believe I missed that."

"Time to wash up!" Greg called out. "And then come put the toppings on your pizza. Let's get this show on the road. We don't want to miss kickoff."

An hour and a half later, Debbie sat high in the stands between Amanda and Greg as the Claymont Mustangs kicked off. Several rows below them sat Julian, Brent, and Monty. Off to the left, the Claymont marching band played the school fight song while the cheerleaders finished a cheer out on the track. Beyond them, Jaxon sat on the home bench at the very end.

He looked so small.

The announcer called out, "Quarterback Dylan Rhodes completed that pass for the Mustangs…" Debbie squinted, trying to recognize the boy behind the face mask. She searched for Madison but didn't see her. She didn't see Kim, Tony, or anyone else from the Palmer family either.

The game was close until the final minutes when the Mustangs lost by a field goal. Jaxon didn't get to play. Dylan did well. He had a good arm and completed most of his passes.

"Too bad," Greg said as they all started down the bleachers. Julian, Monty, and Brent ran out onto the field with the football they brought and passed it back and forth while Amanda, Roger, Greg, and Debbie waited on the track.

Soon the boys started taking turns kicking. Julian got it through the uprights on his first try.

Amanda asked Debbie, "Do you like football?"

"I grew up in Ohio," Debbie answered. "Of course I like football."

Amanda laughed.

"How about you?"

"Well," Amanda said, "I grew up in Ohio too, but I was raised by a single mother who worked every weekend. I never knew anything about the game until I met Roger. I like it now, which is a good thing. Life in our house revolves around sports."

Fifteen minutes later, Jaxon started across the field, carrying his bag over his shoulders. Brent passed him the ball, and Jaxon caught it without much of a reaction. He passed it back and shouted, "Come on, Julian. We're leaving."

When he reached the group of adults, he fixed his gaze on Greg. "Can we go?"

"Sure, sport." Greg put his arm around Jaxon's shoulders and then nudged him, most likely trying to get him to say hello to the other adults.

Debbie said, "Hi, Jaxon. That's great you got to suit up for varsity."

He grunted and didn't saying until Greg nudged him again.

"Thank you for coming to the game," he said, but, like the last time, he didn't meet her eyes.

"You're welcome," Debbie replied.

Amanda gave her a sympathetic look as they walked toward the parking lot. Debbie's face grew warm. Was it that obvious that Jaxon didn't like her? Or was his behavior because he'd taken the model depot and he was afraid Debbie would find out?

She hadn't understood teenage boys twenty-five ago, and she certainly didn't understand them now.

Debbie arrived at the café the next morning at six o'clock to find Paulette and Janet working away, making doughnuts, getting ready for the Fall-iday events. The first train ride would leave the depot at ten, which was when the canteen would open too. "Who's going to staff the canteen?" Debbie asked Janet as she hung up her jacket.

"The volleyball team. Kim arranged it. They needed volunteer hours, plus they're getting a portion of the profits."

As Debbie stepped to the sink to wash her hands, she wondered if Madison would participate. By eight thirty, the café was swamped with customers, and the doughnuts hadn't been boxed yet. Debbie called her mother to see if she could come in and help again. Fifteen minutes later, her mother showed up and Debbie put her to work.

By nine fifteen, everything was back under control. Debbie grabbed a stack of boxes of pumpkin sugar cookies, took them out to the train, and delivered them to the volunteer, who sat in the first seat, bundled in a coat and scarf that seemed more than what she needed. The morning wasn't very cold.

Then she went back to the café and grabbed two jugs of cider, put them in a box with enough cups and napkins, and took those out to the train too. The volunteer hadn't moved.

"Are you feeling all right?" Debbie asked.

"Yes," the woman said. "I just need to warm up."

Next Debbie returned to the café for the doughnuts and asked Mom to help her. Together they carried the boxes out to the east side of the depot, where the canteen had been positioned. Not only was Madison there, but so was Eileen.

"Eileen, are you going to help sell doughnuts?" Debbie asked.

Eileen smiled. "No, I'm going to go on the train and reminisce about the old days. Sofia's coming with me."

"Oh, that's great. Have you heard how Gayle is today?"

"Much better," Eileen said. "She was discharged to her cousin's house yesterday, but the doctor insists she stay put for a couple of days. Trudy is staying at the cousin's house too, and she picked up Ray this morning so he could spend time with Gayle."

"That's so good to hear." Debbie watched as Madison, Kim, five other teenage girls, and the volleyball coach arrived from opposite directions at the same time.

"I'll give you instructions in a minute," Kim said to the coach. Then she turned to Debbie. "Our volunteer on the train isn't feeling well and needs to go home. Can you go in her place and pass out the cookies when you reach the Bowerston Depot? That's the halfway point for the trip."

Debbie turned to her mom. "Do you want to go?"

"No, you should," Mom said. "I can help in the café for a couple more hours."

"Are you sure?"

"Absolutely." Mom nodded vigorously. "You've been working so hard. It would be great for you to have a break."

"Janet's been working just as hard, if not harder." Debbie turned to Kim. "I'll go ask her if she wants the job."

Janet wanted to stay at the café. "You go. We'll be fine. Just hurry back when the train arrives. We might get some of the passengers as customers."

Debbie agreed and thanked her friend. Then she found her mom again. "Are you sure you're all right working for a couple more hours?"

"Absolutely. I know how much you enjoy train rides. Have fun!"

Debbie headed straight for the train. Mom was right. She loved train rides. One of her favorite childhood memories was riding the Christmas train from the Dennison Depot.

She bounded up the steps of the train as "We'll Meet Again" played over the sound system.

A shiver shot through her as she listened to the words. She had a shared experience with so many widows and fiancées whose loved ones didn't return home from war. Everyone hoped they'd meet again, but it didn't always happen, at least in this lifetime.

She was thankful that Sofia's parents did meet again and were able to reunite, with little Sofia, in Dennison. What a blessing for all of them.

Debbie organized the refreshments and greeted each passenger as they came up the steps. Sofia and Eileen were last and sat down across from Debbie at the front of the car as the chorus of the song played one more time.

"I've always loved this song," Eileen said. "It brought us all hope during the war, just like so many other songs did."

"I really love it too," Debbie said.

"Have you learned anything more about my family?" Sofia asked as they waited for the train to start.

"Yes," Debbie said. "I have no idea if it's relevant or not." She told Sofia about Anna and her animosity toward Bob and Marguerite.

"Interesting," Sofia said. "I've thought more about what the volunteer at the library said about my birth certificate. I always felt as if my parents had secrets, but maybe everyone feels that way."

Debbie never felt as if her parents did, but she didn't want to say that to Sofia.

Sofia sighed. "I think one of the reasons kids teased me, besides what they may have heard from their parents, is because I looked nothing like my father. He was tall and blond and big-boned. I was petite and had dark hair. But I figured I got all my genes from Mama. Perhaps there was a reason I was hesitant to take a DNA test and didn't feel as if I should until after Mama passed away."

"Hopefully, the truth will be revealed," Eileen said. "Both about your origins and whatever your mother hid."

"I hope so," Sofia replied.

Debbie reached across the aisle and patted Sofia's arm. "I agree."

When the whistle blew, Eileen said, "Isn't this exciting?"

"Yes," Sofia said. "It reminds me of when Mama and I first arrived in Dennison."

"You remember?" Debbie asked. "How old were you?"

"Two. It's one of those memories that I'm not sure if I actually remember, or if Mama told me about it so many times that it just feels as if I do. Some people say children can remember things that young. Others disagree."

"What do you remember?" Debbie asked.

"Well, first I'll tell you what I absolutely don't remember but what Mama told me over the years. She was ill for nearly the entire trip across the Atlantic. I stayed by her side, curled up on the lower bunk we had. I was hungry, and there was food in the dining hall, more food than I'd ever seen before and more than Mama had seen since the war began, but she was too sick to get us there. So I was hungry and afraid until other war brides began bringing me food and taking me to the bathroom and changing my clothes and caring for Mama too. Finally, by the time we reached New York, Mama felt better and took me up on deck. She pointed to the Statue of Liberty and taught me to say the word *liberty* along with *Hello Daddy, I love you, I'm happy to be in America*, and other words and phrases in English.

"I don't remember our trip west on the train to Ohio either, but Mama felt fine by then, and she said she was amazed by the vastness of the United States and the beauty of the scenery. And yet it made her miss France and the train rides through the farm country that she took her first year away from home from Paris to Marseilles, where her father owned a shipping company. After the war started, she didn't return home until her mother was terminally ill in 1961. Her father had already passed away, and there was no one else to care for her mother."

The whistle blew again, and the train began moving slowly. "What I do remember is Daddy when we arrived, right here at the Dennison Depot." She pointed out the window to her right past Eileen. Then she turned her attention back to Debbie. "Daddy had flowers for Mama and a balloon for me. He was a giant of a man. Six foot five and two hundred and thirty pounds. I remember how tightly he hugged us. I remember being sandwiched between Mama and Daddy and feeling so safe." Sofia smiled.

"What a beautiful memory," Debbie said. "What else do you remember?"

"Not much for the next few years. I know, from what Mama said later, that it wasn't an easy transition for her. I can imagine how hard it was, because by the time I was six or seven, people sometimes made rude comments, calling her a frog and 'Frenchie.'"

Debbie winced.

"Others were very kind and made all the difference for her." Sofia patted Eileen's leg. "But I think there were a handful of people who resented my mother for whatever reasons. Mama, Daddy, and I went to see *Lady and the Tramp* in Uhrichsville, the first movie I ever saw. We hardly ever splurged. Daddy had grown up during the Depression. Mama wasn't as affected by that, but she knew more than any of us what it was like to be poor and hungry during the war. Both saved more than they spent, so it was a real treat to finally go to a movie, something my classmates often did. That evening, as we came out of the theater, a woman glared at Daddy and said, 'What a fitting movie for the two of you to see. You're both tramps.'"

Debbie groaned. "That's horrible."

It was Eileen's turn to pat Sofia's leg. "I'm so sorry someone said that at all, but especially in front of you, as a child."

Sofia gaped at her. "You knew about that?"

Eileen nodded. "Your mother told me."

"Was she upset? Because she didn't act as if she was. She didn't say anything, but Daddy took both of our hands and said to the woman, 'That was uncalled for. If you have a problem with me, address me. But leave my loved ones alone.'"

"Yes, your mother was upset," Eileen said. "I'm guessing your father was too. Back then, we still said 'Sticks and stones may break my bones, but words will never hurt me.' But we didn't believe it, even though we repeated it. Words hurt horribly."

"I know they hurt me," Sofia said. "I wondered why a woman I'd never met would call my parents tramps. They didn't say a word about the encounter after it happened, just as I never told them about the kids who said Mama and I should go back to France. Both made me feel as if we didn't belong, although I knew Daddy did belong. Dennison was his hometown."

"Speaking of…" Eileen pointed out the window. Was she changing the subject on purpose? "I haven't been on a train ride since Madison was tiny, and that was the Christmas train. Look at our town. Isn't it lovely?"

Debbie gazed past Sofia and Eileen as the train rolled past the sign in the trainyard.

"'Dreamsville,'" Sofia read. "By and large that was true for us. This was the land of plenty, Mama always said after the war and all that followed it in Paris. And she said we had our very own knight in shining armor too—Daddy."

The train picked up speed. The leaves of the maple, oak, and buckeye trees throughout town were ablaze in fiery reds, oranges, and yellows against the brick and wooden buildings from the early 1900s.

When she was in high school, Debbie scoffed at the "Dreamsville" moniker for Dennison. How could the town of just over two thousand people be anyone's dream? She couldn't wait to leave. But she got it now. She finally understood the importance of community. And of that, Dennison had plenty. Regardless of the opposition Marguerite faced, she'd found support in Dennison too.

The song "I'll Be Seeing You" came over the sound system, and Debbie smiled as Billie Holiday sang of the old familiar places. She turned to look out the window. Dennison was her familiar place.

The train soon left the city limits. The countryside of fields and wooded areas practically sparkled under the October sun. Debbie's heart grew full as she soaked in the view, and yet she still felt pained that someone could be so rude all those years ago to the Jennings family.

Who was the woman who confronted the young family outside the theater that day? And did that abuse have anything to do with the missing model depot and painting today?

CHAPTER FOURTEEN

*A*n hour and a half later, Debbie stepped into the café with the empty cookie boxes. She smiled at Paulette, who was delivering sandwiches to an older couple, and then continued into the kitchen.

"How'd everything go?" Debbie's mom asked as she grabbed a carton of half-and-half from the cooler.

"Great! Both the cookies and the cider were a big hit." Debbie held up the empty boxes. "How have things been here?"

"Steady." Mom smiled.

Janet stood at the grill, flipping a cheese sandwich. "Hey," Debbie called out. "Everyone loved the pumpkin sugar cookies. We should put them on the menu for the rest of the month."

Janet held up her spatula and grinned. "Sounds like a good plan."

Debbie gathered the boxes of cookies and cider for the next ride, placed them on the dolly, and delivered them to the next volunteer. Then she wheeled the empty dolly around the depot to the canteen. Several people who had just disembarked from the train were in line to buy doughnuts. Debbie hoped they'd save the doughnuts for later and head into the café for lunch.

There was Jaxon. He didn't see Debbie, and she decided not to call to him.

She stood on her tiptoes to see if Madison was still selling doughnuts. She didn't see her. The sound of raised voices behind her caught Debbie's attention. She pivoted.

Madison and Dylan stood at the edge of the parking lot.

"No, I don't want to talk," Madison practically shouted.

Dylan crossed his arms. "Just for a minute."

"Maddie!" Eileen stepped out of the doughnut line. Sofia followed her. Jaxon's head popped up from the middle of the line.

Dylan shook his head as if in disgust.

Madison glanced at her great-grandmother and then faced Dylan. Both Eileen and Jaxon stepped off the curb onto the asphalt. Debbie hesitated a moment and then crossed the street, pushing the dolly in front of her. "Madison!" she called. "I need your help getting more doughnuts from the café."

Madison squinted at Debbie. "Okay." She turned back to Dylan. "See you later." Then she walked to Debbie.

"Lead the way," Debbie said.

When they reached the front door to the depot, Madison stopped. "Thank you. I can't believe he showed up like that, in front of everyone."

"What did he want?"

"To talk about the night of the accident. He said everyone ganged up on him and said it was his fault."

Debbie raised her eyebrows. "Why would people say that?"

"Because it's the truth." Madison started walking across the lobby of the depot and toward the café. "He went fast over the tracks on purpose, to get airborne, and then he turned left at the last minute. He told everyone he was going the speed limit and signaled." Madison opened the door for Debbie. "I can't lie for him."

"Of course not," Debbie murmured as she wheeled the dolly through the door. "Come into the kitchen with me, and we'll load the dolly up with doughnuts. I'll go back out to the canteen with you in case Dylan hangs around."

Debbie's mom said hello to Madison as she cleared the table closest to the door. Then Paulette said hello from behind the counter. Madison responded to each with a smile and a polite, "Hello."

When they reached the kitchen, Janet gave Madison a big smile. "How are the sales going out there?"

"Great," Madison said. "Everyone loves your doughnuts."

"We're taking another load out," Debbie said.

"Perfect." Janet mimicked crossing off an item on an imaginary list. "That was my next task."

Debbie handed Madison a stack of boxes.

"Does your mom work here all the time?" Madison asked.

"No. She just fills in when we're in a pinch."

"How about Mrs. Connor?"

"She does work here all the time."

Madison put the boxes on the dolly. "Do you plan to hire anyone else?"

Debbie grabbed three more boxes of doughnuts from the counter. "I'm not sure. Why do you ask?"

Madison shrugged.

"Are you looking for a job?" Debbie asked.

Madison put the boxes on top of the others and then stepped to the back of the dolly. "I'm not sure."

"What about volleyball?"

"I'm going to be sitting on the bench."

"Because of the accident?"

Madison nodded. "Because of my concussion. My dad won't let me play." She turned the dolly around, and Debbie followed her as she pushed it out of the café.

Once they were in the lobby, Debbie took a couple of quick steps and caught up with Madison. "What are you interested in besides volleyball and volunteering at Good Shepherd?"

"I like the idea of designing apps," Madison said. "I think it would be fun to learn how to make them. Or learn computer programming."

They reached the depot exit, and Madison slowed so Debbie could open the door. Madison sailed through, obviously enjoying piloting the dolly. As they got nearer to the canteen, Debbie saw Kristy at the end of the line.

Kristy waved, and Debbie waved back. Hadn't Kristy said she'd like to mentor high school girls? Madison could use a mentor.

But would Kristy be the best mentor for Madison? Debbie wasn't sure if either one was trustworthy.

After they restocked the canteen with doughnuts, Madison took her place with her teammates and Debbie stepped to the side to scan the area for Dylan. He was nowhere in sight. Eileen and Sofia had made their way to the bench in the corner of the depot, and Jaxon was now first in line. Debbie watched as Madison grinned at him and asked what he wanted.

His face grew red. "A dozen, please."

"All for you?" she teased.

"I wish," he muttered.

She counted out twelve doughnuts from a big box and placed them into a smaller one.

Jaxon dug a bill from his front pocket and handed it to Madison. She made change and gave it to him. "See you later."

He gave her a quick nod and turned toward Debbie.

"Hi, Jaxon," she said.

He startled but then said, "Oh, hi."

"Enjoy the doughnuts."

"We will," he said.

"Are you all watching the game?" The Ohio State game would start in half an hour.

He nodded. "With Brent's family."

"Nice. Tell everyone hello for me."

"I will. Dad said to tell you hello if I saw you."

"Thank you," she said. "See you soon."

He waved and started down the street. He seemed so meek and mild by himself, without his father, brother, or any friends around. And he had spoken to her more in that brief exchange than he had in the last week.

Debbie approached Kristy, who was now in the middle of the line. "How are you today?"

"Good. I was out for a walk, and I saw that the canteen is open. I thought doughnuts would be a nice surprise for Carson. He's working away on a deadline."

"Where's BG?"

"With Carson, napping. I didn't want to disturb her."

"Mom's in the café, if you want to stop in and say hello."

"I'll do that," Kristy said. "It would do me good to be around some other people. Carson's having a writing weekend."

"I'll see you in a few minutes." As Debbie turned away, she thanked God—for the hundredth time—for her job. It was more than she dreamed it could be. She was living in Dreamsville. Yes, the incident with Madison and Dylan had been disturbing, but she had been able to intervene. And the train ride, including hearing Sofia's story, had been invigorating. Owning and operating the café with Janet, plus all the interactions with people around town, gave her a sort of energy she'd never experienced before. It was so different than her corporate management job. She'd found that draining by the time she resigned. But serving others in Dennison had made her feel alive again.

She stopped to check in on Eileen and Sofia on the bench. Each had a doughnut in one hand and a cup of coffee in the other. "How are you two doing?"

"All right," Eileen said. "Thank you for intervening on behalf of Madison."

"My pleasure." Debbie leaned against the dolly.

Sofia placed her doughnut on the napkin on her lap. "I guess bullying is timeless, isn't it?"

"I'm afraid so," Debbie said. "Although I think more people are aware of it now and refuse to tolerate it. In most circumstances I think it's easier to stand up against it."

"I hope you're right," Sofia said.

Ten minutes later, Debbie's mom sat at a table eating a sandwich and a bowl of tomato bisque. Debbie saw Kristy come in with a half-dozen-size box of doughnuts and wave at her mom. "Mind if I join you, Mrs. Albright?"

"Please do, but only if you call me Becca. Mrs. Albright was one thing when you were all in high school, but now hardly anyone calls me that, and it makes me feel ancient."

Kristy smiled. "Thank you, Becca." She leaned forward. "Did you hear about Debbie's birthday dinner at our house?"

"Yes," Mom said. "It sounds like fun."

"I'm sending out invitation texts this afternoon to make it all official. Carson is going to fix a Mediterranean chicken skillet. I'm going to decorate with an autumn motif. And Janet is going to make the cake—top secret of course."

Debbie chuckled as she approached with a menu and handed it to Kristy. "Do you mind if I join you two for a minute?" she asked.

"Sure," Mom said as Kristy said, "No problem."

Debbie slid next to her mother.

Kristy said, "What do you want to talk about?"

"Oh, I don't have anything in mind," Debbie said. "I just don't want the focus to be on me."

Kristy laughed. "Well, I have something I want to talk about."

Debbie's eyebrows shot upward.

"Do you remember I mentioned I'd like to mentor high school girls?"

Debbie nodded.

"What do you think the best way to go about that would be? Talk with someone at the high school? Maybe one of the counselors?"

"Yes," Debbie said. "I'd call the office. The secretary will direct you to the right person."

"I'll do that Monday," Kristy said. "They must have some sort of program in place. I imagine I'd need to have a background check and that sort of thing."

The subject turned to the birthday dinner again, and Debbie soon returned to the kitchen. Maybe Kristy would end up mentoring Madison after all.

Mom left after she finished her lunch, and Kristy moved to the counter to drink her coffee and scroll through her phone. Soon both Paulette and Janet went home too, and Debbie began cleaning up, stopping to make mostly to-go drinks for people waiting for the train or arriving to visit the museum.

At one forty-five, Madison came into the café, carrying a stack of empty doughnut boxes.

"Thank you," Debbie said, stepping from behind the counter to take the boxes. "Are you all done?"

"Yes. We sold out."

"Perfect." Debbie smiled. "How about a drink? On the house."

Madison rubbed her hands together. "Can I have hot chocolate? It's getting chilly out there."

"Coming right up."

Madison sat next to Kristy, and Debbie introduced the two. "We went to school together. Kristy and her husband moved back to Dennison a few weeks ago."

"Nice to meet you," Madison said.

"Likewise," Kristy answered.

"Madison is a freshman at the high school," Debbie added and then turned around to make the cocoa.

When Debbie delivered the drink, Kristy was asking Madison what her interests were. Debbie stepped back near the kitchen, but without any equipment operating she could hear the conversation.

"I really enjoy working with the seniors at Good Shepherd," Madison answered. "I lead a chair exercise class three days a week. I saw it online, and it looked like fun. But I'm also interested in programming. I'd like to develop an app for seniors to help keep them moving."

"Impressive," Kristy said. Debbie silently agreed. Kristy continued. "I have a degree in computer science from Ohio State and work in the gaming industry."

"Wow."

"It's a lot of fun," Kristy said. "But I've played around some with designing apps. A list app. A chores app. A dog care app. That sort of thing."

"Cool," Madison said.

"Have you looked to see what kind of exercise apps are out there?"

Madison nodded. "I have, and I think I've gotten some good ideas from some of them. I'd like to kind of make it a game they would like."

"I think that's a great idea," Kristy said. "You could bring a lot of people joy, along with healing, with a program like that." She smiled. "Maybe I could help you."

Madison wrapped both hands around her cup. "How?"

"Well, I was thinking about talking with someone at your school about mentoring high school girls in science or math, in designing in particular. Once I find out what the process is, I'll let them know we might be a match. If you'd like me to do that."

Madison beamed. "I'd love that."

Debbie began cleaning the grill and could no longer hear the two. Madison and Kristy both seemed so normal, so caring and motivated and even driven. And yet one of them—or both—could be a thief.

At least she hadn't suggested Kristy mentor Madison. That had happened all on its own.

The energy Debbie gained from her job had waned by the time Sunday's service ended and she chatted with other congregants outside. It didn't help that gray clouds filled the sky and a cold wind blew. After she'd chatted with Ray and Eileen and Kristy and Carson, she felt downright tired.

Greg and the boys had left as soon as the service ended. They joined Brent, Monty, and Roger for what would likely turn out to be a rainy hike on the Tappan Dam Trailhead.

Relieved Mom and Dad hadn't invited anyone else to Sunday dinner, she arrived at their house ready for comfort food and a chance to relax. She wasn't disappointed. Mom had prepared old-fashioned meat loaf, mashed potatoes and gravy, roasted carrots, and fresh peach cobbler for dessert. Mom had been saving the last of the peaches she'd purchased in early September for one last cobbler of the season.

"No wonder your Sunday dinners are famous," Debbie said as she finished the last bite of cobbler. "What did I do to deserve parents like you?"

Mom laughed while Dad stood and took a bow. "I peeled the peaches."

They all laughed.

"Before you go," Mom said, "I found a box of your things in the spare bedroom closet."

"Really? I thought I'd gotten all my things years ago."

"I thought so too. It was pushed into the corner. I'll be right back." Mom left and returned a few minutes later with a cardboard shoebox.

"Did you look inside?" Debbie asked.

Mom shook her head. "I was tempted but resisted." She grinned.

Debbie laughed as she took the lid off. "I have no secrets, I can assure you." She picked up the first item. A diary from middle school. "I take that back. No doubt there are all sorts of secrets in here."

"Believe me," Mom said, "I don't want to read it."

Debbie laughed again. "But you'll miss all the middle-school drama."

"I lived through it once," Mom said. "There's no need to relive it."

"I agree." Debbie set the diary on the table. Next, she pulled out an unlit round candle layered with blue, purple, and lavender wax. "I remember this. Janet gave it to me when we were juniors. I wondered what happened to it."

Next were a couple of birthday cards, one from Janet and one from Kristy. Finally, in the very bottom of the box, was a pair of earrings. Gold hoops. She held them up. "I can't believe it. These are the earrings Janet gave me for my seventeenth birthday." Her voice turned raspy. "The ones I thought Kristy stole."

CHAPTER FIFTEEN

*A*s Debbie walked home from her mom and dad's in the drizzling rain, her hand around the earrings in the pocket of her jacket, she thought of the time Kristy was accused of taking someone's textbook from government class. Kristy was offended and demanded that the vice principal search her locker. The textbook wasn't in the locker and didn't turn up until the end of the year. Someone had crammed it behind other books in the library. No one ever knew who did it.

It was a smart move for Kristy to demand the principal search her locker, but it didn't mean that she hadn't taken the textbook and hidden it in the library. That was what Debbie had always thought happened, mainly because she thought Kristy had stolen her earrings too.

The same could be true of Madison. She'd asked Kim to search her room, but that didn't mean she hadn't taken the model train depot and the painting. It just meant she hadn't stashed them in her room.

Debbie strained to remember exactly what happened with the earrings twenty-seven years ago, almost to the day. Had she tucked them in one of the cards and put them in the box? Then, when she couldn't find the earrings, she'd blamed Kristy who, besides Janet, had been the only other person in her bedroom. Back then, Janet and Kristy came over nearly every day after school if they didn't have something going on. Mom worked part-time and almost always had some kind of snack around. And if not, there were always plenty of ingredients to make something, which Janet enjoyed doing.

"Debbie!"

She turned. Trudy, Gayle's daughter, stood on the porch of a Victorian house across the street.

Debbie waved. "Hi, Trudy!" She crossed the street. "How's your mother?"

"Much better. I'll take her to the doctor Tuesday, and then hopefully I can take her home on Wednesday. Want to come in? Uncle Ray is here. Everyone's in the living room."

"Yes," Debbie said. "I'd like that." She hurried up the porch steps and flipped her hood back, flicking the water off it once she reached the door. Then she zipped the pocket of her jacket with the earrings in it and stepped inside.

Trudy put out her hand for Debbie's jacket and hung it on the coat tree. Then Debbie followed her into the living room. Gayle was stretched out on a recliner, her casted arm resting on a pillow, and Ray sat near her in his wheelchair.

"Hello," Debbie said to both of them, and then addressed Gayle. "How are you doing today?"

"Good, thank you." She pointed to a wingback chair. "Please, sit."

"Would you like coffee?" Trudy asked. "It's already made, but I'm afraid it's decaf. That's better for Mother right now."

"That would be great," Debbie said. "Thank you. Is your cousin around?"

Gayle shook her head. "She's at her daughter's for Sunday dinner. She's given us the run of the house."

Ray smiled. "I don't know what we'd have done without her this week."

"Neither do I," Trudy said as she came into the living room with a mug. She handed it to Debbie. "Mother, I'm going to start a pot of soup for supper. Holler if you need anything."

A few minutes later, as Debbie drank her coffee, Gayle said, "I've had a lot of time to think the last few days. Funny, the things that come to mind when one has uninterrupted time."

Debbie leaned forward in her chair and cradled her mug. "What have you been thinking about?"

"The Jennings family. Bob and Marguerite and Sofia. Years ago, Marguerite seemed so confident, besides being fascinating, but now, as an old woman, I can see that it must have been a difficult transition for her. I wonder how much time she and Bob actually had together in France. Arriving in the American Midwest with a two-year-old in an entirely new culture—it must have been a shock. She was so tiny, so petite. I remember wondering if she worked at being so thin, but now I think it must have been a lack of food during the war and after. I've read there was a real scarcity of adequate nutrition in Europe."

Debbie thought for a moment. Then she said, "Sofia said her mother told her that there was more food on the ship coming over here than she'd seen since the war began. Unfortunately, Marguerite was seasick the entire trip."

"Well," Gayle said, "that could have contributed to her frailty." She turned to Ray. "Do you remember when she and Sofia arrived?"

He nodded. "I didn't go to the train station, but Bob brought them by a couple of days later and introduced them. I was staying with Mother and Father at the time, still recuperating. I was on the porch—I think it was spring. Bob held Sofia, and Marguerite walked beside him. I'd never seen him so happy, and he was one of the happiest people I knew."

"Do you remember people gossiping about how Sofia didn't look a thing like him?" Gayle asked. "That they doubted she was his child?"

Ray shook his head.

Gayle paused a moment. "Maybe I'm not remembering right."

"You are," Debbie said. "Yesterday, Sofia told me kids said that to her. Most likely they heard it from their parents."

Gayle pursed her lips. "That makes me sad for Sofia."

"It's not that she doesn't think Bob was her biological father. It's just that she always felt there were a lot of secrets about her mother's life in France," Debbie said.

"Well," Ray said, "I can tell you that Bob was her real dad in every way that counts. I've never seen a man more devoted than Bob Jennings, especially during a time when fathers weren't as hands-on as they are now."

Gayle shifted in her recliner, adjusting the position of her arm. "I wonder if Bob was injured in the war," Gayle said.

"I never heard any such thing," Ray replied. "I think he made it through physically unscathed."

"If he was hurt, I doubt it would have been talked about around town. He was a war hero. But people *did* gossip about Marguerite."

Ray grasped the arms of his wheelchair, as if he might get up. He didn't, but he did lean forward. "Gayle, you make the townspeople of Dennison sound like horrible gossips. They were, and are, good people."

"Of course they were and are. Absolutely. There were just a few of them that were gossips back then. And the more I think of it, the more I think Anna was at the heart of it. She'd convinced herself that Bob loved her when that was never the case. She was horribly jealous of Marguerite. I think she was the one who spread the rumors. I think by the time Minnie died, Minnie realized it too, but by then she valued Marguerite and appreciated her. And she should have. It was Marguerite and Bob who cared for Minnie when she was dying."

"I remember that," Ray said. "Minnie spent the last couple of months of her life in their spare bedroom."

"One never would have guessed that Bob Jennings would ever marry someone like Marguerite, but they made a good team," Gayle said. "I could tell when I babysat for Sofia. The home was peaceful. Sofia was well cared for. One time I heard Marguerite get angry at Bob—I can't even remember what it was about. Some sort of misunderstanding. He listened to her, and they hashed it out. That's what marriages should be about, right? Listening and resolving problems. Taking care of others. Loving each other."

Debbie agreed. "Others can't always see that if they don't know the couple, can they?"

"That's right," Gayle said. "I hope Sofia looks back on her parents' lives and sees their love for each other, and for her. No doubt, both Marguerite and Bob carried lasting wounds from the war that no one could see, but they also had a lot to contribute to our community. The pieces they made and painted for the model train display were the least of what they did."

"What are some of the other things they did?" Debbie asked.

"Well, in the time I was still around, before I left for college, Bob helped repair houses in the neighborhood for the elderly. One time, he helped Father fix our gutters. Another time, when Mother was ill and I had school finals, Marguerite brought over a casserole that tasted like chicken cordon bleu. It was delicious. And Marguerite grew flowers and took bouquets to the neighbor women, along with baked goods she made."

Debbie thought of the *galette des rois* that Kim remembered Marguerite making at Christmastime. Then she thought about the story Sofia told about the woman confronting the family outside of the theater after they'd watched *Lady and the Tramp*. She told Gayle and Ray the story. "Do you think that could have been Anna?"

"Perhaps," Gayle said. "You know back then, when she was rude to Marguerite, I thought she was odd and badly behaved. But now I wonder if she had some sort of mental illness."

Debbie agreed that could have been a possibility and then stood. "I should let you rest." She picked up her mug. "I'll go tell Trudy goodbye before I leave."

She headed down the hall to the kitchen, which was nicely remodeled with white cabinets, granite countertops, and an eating nook. She'd have to ask Greg if he did it. "Thank you, Trudy, for the coffee," Debbie said, making her way to the sink.

Trudy looked up from the island where she was chopping vegetables.

"You're welcome," she said. "I'll most likely return in a couple of months. I told Mom I'd bring her back so she can see Uncle Ray. Those two can't seem to get enough of each other sometimes."

"No doubt," Debbie said. They both probably feared losing the other. "I've really enjoyed getting to know your mother. She's a gem."

"Absolutely," Trudy said. "I still shake at the thought of that accident. I'm so thankful she's going to be all right."

"So am I." Debbie smiled at Trudy, catching her gaze. Trudy smiled back, revealing the same dimples as her mother had.

Debbie returned to the living room and told Ray goodbye first. "No doubt I'll see you in a day or two."

"I hope so," he said.

Then she told Gayle goodbye. "Thank you for the stories about Marguerite. Ray will have to let you know when we find the model depot and painting."

Gayle's eyebrows shot up. "'When'?"

"Yes," Debbie said. "I'm not giving up."

Gayle nodded. "Good for you."

"It sounds as if I'll be seeing you in a couple of months," Debbie said.

"I hope so," Gayle said. "It does me good to see Ray and spend time in Dennison. I'm looking forward to my next visit."

Debbie leaned down and gave her a soft hug, avoiding her broken arm. "Have a good trip home."

A block away, as Debbie continued toward home, the rain started again, and she pulled her hood over her head. Then she remembered the earrings and unzipped her pocket. She put her hand inside, and clasped the earrings again. Did Kristy remember Debbie asking her all those years ago if she knew what happened to the earrings when they went missing? Did Kristy realize Debbie asking her was a veiled accusation that Kristy had taken them? Did she need to apologize to Kristy now?

She cringed as she trudged through a small pile of wet leaves on the sidewalk, thinking about Kristy apologizing to her about the way she'd acted during the last couple years of high school. Kristy had been standoffish, but she had reason to be. Her mother had terminal cancer.

Debbie swallowed hard. She needed to do the right thing. It didn't matter if Kristy took the depot or not. Either way, she owed Kristy an apology about the earrings.

Debbie passed the Jennings house and the arc of ivy that grew across the sidewalk at the edge of their property. She imagined Bob building the frame and putting it in place and then, perhaps, Marguerite coaxing the ivy up and over and then down the other side of the frame. She would call Kristy tomorrow and see if they could go for a walk or have coffee. She needed to talk to her before the birthday party. The sooner the better.

Debbie felt unsettled as she remembered being so sure, for all these years, that Kristy had taken the earrings. She reached her own house and climbed the stairs slowly, thinking of Sofia being sure that her mother had kept secrets from her.

As Debbie unlocked her door, she vowed to be as honest as possible. She'd start by calling Kristy. Tomorrow.

CHAPTER SIXTEEN

The next morning, after readying the café to open, Debbie and Janet sat side by side at the counter, waiting five more minutes before turning the sign. They both had their hands wrapped around cups of coffee. Debbie thought about telling Janet that she'd found the earrings she'd accused Kristy of stealing all those years ago but decided not to. Not yet.

Instead, she asked, "Any chance Ian might stop by today? I have a question for him."

"As a matter of fact..." Janet checked her phone. "He's on his way here."

When Ian arrived, Janet had a cup of tea and a scone with orange marmalade ready for him.

"Thank you, love." He gave her a kiss across the counter and then sat down.

Janet motioned to Debbie, who poured a cup of coffee for their first customer. "Guess who has a question for you."

Ian groaned.

"Prepare yourself," Debbie said. "I'll be right back."

After she delivered the coffee and cinnamon roll, she stood across the counter from Ian and spoke softly. "So, Dylan Rhodes volunteers at Good Shepherd. He was there last Monday afternoon when Ray's painting went missing."

"You think he's a suspect?"

Debbie put the coffeepot back on the burner. "He was in the museum the evening the depot went missing, remember? Did you question him?"

"I did broach the subject with him, both about the depot and the painting, after I questioned him about the accident."

Debbie winced. That was a lot for Dylan to deal with all at once. "And?"

"He says he doesn't know a thing about either item." Ian took a sip of tea. "He said he heard Madison mention the model depot that night but that he left right away after that. And he said he doesn't even know who Ray Zink is. He only sees the same two residents—women—every week."

"Do you think he's telling the truth?"

"I have no reason to think he isn't." Ian spread the marmalade on his scone. "I don't see what his motive would be to take either item."

Debbie had thought the same thing about Dylan's lack of a motive.

Another customer came into the café, and Debbie grabbed a menu. "Thank you," she said to Ian and then headed back out on the floor.

A half hour later, after Ian left, as Debbie grabbed an order in the kitchen, she said to Janet, "I keep forgetting to tell you that Sofia is fine with you investigating her family."

Janet flipped an omelet. "You told her Esther at the library thought it might be a birth certificate from an adoption?"

"I did."

"And she's not freaked out about it?"

"No, she's not."

"Cool." Janet smiled. "Because here comes Harry, along with Patricia. I'm going to ask if she has any ideas about how to figure this out."

Once Patricia and Harry had settled at their regular table, with Crosby on the floor, Debbie took their order. It was the usual. A peppermint mocha and a pastry for Patricia—which never changed—and Harry's most recent preference. Black coffee, two eggs over medium, bacon, hash browns and a biscuit.

After Debbie put the order in, she pointed to the dining room and told Janet, "Go talk to Patricia about the birth certificate. I'll get their breakfast ready."

"All right." Janet wiped her hands on her apron and headed out to the floor.

Debbie started the hash browns and then the bacon. A few minutes later, as she was frying the eggs, Janet came back into the kitchen.

"What did Patricia say?" Debbie asked.

"That she'll look into it. She has access to a public records database. She said she's not sure what the process would have been in 1947, but because Bob was a US citizen, Sofia would have automatically become one. She would have needed a US birth certificate, which is what we assumed. Getting a birth certificate for a foreign-born child of a US citizen would be the same process for an adoptee, so the woman at the library could have been simply pointing out that it resembled an adoptive certificate, even if it wasn't. Or maybe Sofia didn't have a French birth certificate."

"Why wouldn't she?"

"Patricia said some births never got registered in Europe during both world wars, especially if the baby wasn't born in a hospital. Or perhaps Marguerite wasn't able to get a copy of the birth certificate. So much went on after the war with displaced people and unaccounted for deceased people. A lot of paperwork fell through the cracks."

"I hadn't thought of that," Debbie said.

"I wonder if anyone at the newspaper ever did a story on Marguerite," Janet mused.

"Sofia never mentioned anything like that."

"I think I'll go back to the library and dig some more in the newspaper microfiche. Her story would have made a great feature on the fiftieth anniversary of VE Day."

"Just think," Debbie said. "It's only a couple of years until the eightieth anniversary."

"I hope Ray will still be alive." Janet flipped the eggs.

Debbie's stomach nearly hit the floor. She didn't want to think about Ray not being around.

More customers came in, and the morning grew busy. Just before eight, Patricia left for her office. Harry stayed around for another half hour then put his hat on, and Debbie gave him her biggest smile. "Have a great day!"

"Oh, I will," he said. "Every day is a great day."

As he stood and collected Crosby's leash, she thought of what a treasure Harry was to the town. He cared deeply for others, humans and animals, and most noticeably for Patricia and for Crosby. He was a great example of someone who had lived exceptionally in the everyday moments of his life, as both a porter for the railroad and then as a conductor. And through his years in retirement. He could have simply called 911 the night of the crash, but instead, after he called 911, he ran out to help, having no idea what he'd find.

Harry tipped his hat to Debbie as he stepped toward the door. "See you tomorrow."

"See you then." Debbie's heart swelled. She dreaded the morning when she wouldn't see Harry for breakfast in the café. If only he could live forever. If only all her senior citizen friends could.

She sighed and returned to her work.

Paulette arrived at nine, alleviating Debbie's quick trips from the kitchen to the floor to the counter and back to the floor. Once the breakfast rush ended, business slowed, and a lunch rush never materialized, which sometimes happened on Mondays. Paulette went home, and Janet left a little before two. When Debbie had finished her tasks, she sat at the far table to tackle the books.

A half hour later, someone knocked on the café door.

Debbie hesitated but then stood and walked to the door. Madison peered through the window, and when she saw Debbie, she waved and said something.

Debbie couldn't hear her, but she opened the door. "Why aren't you at practice?"

"It's too hard to be there but not be able to play."

Debbie swung the door wide. "Come on in. Would you like some hot cocoa?"

"Could I have a pumpkin spice latte instead?" Madison sat down on a stool.

That was what Kristy had ordered on Saturday. "Of course."

Debbie stepped behind the counter and began making Madison's drink. "Will you be able to sit on the bench during games?"

"I could," Madison answered. "But I don't want to waste my after-school time just sitting around. I'd rather get a job."

Debbie finished the latte, poured it into a to-go cup, and handed it to Madison. "Where do you hope to get a job?"

Madison wrapped both hands around the cup. "Here."

"Here?"

Madison nodded. "Are you hiring?"

Debbie leaned against the counter. Madison knew the café closed at two and that there were no after-school hours available. "Are we hiring..." She smiled at Madison. "I don't think so, but I'll talk with Janet about it. We might need help on Saturdays, but it would only be occasionally."

Madison wrinkled her nose but then said, "That might work."

Debbie smiled at her. "I'll ask Janet. I'll be right back."

She went into the kitchen and made the call. Janet agreed they could use help on Saturday. "That would keep us from relying on your mom when we're in a pinch. Plus, it would give you, Paulette, and me a chance to schedule regular Saturdays off. Are you sure about Madison being the best person to hire?"

"Yes," Debbie said.

"Is she still a suspect?"

"Technically, yes," Debbie admitted. "But my intuition says she's not the culprit. I think if she was, the model depot would have shown up in the museum by now. And the painting would be back at Good Shepherd." Debbie thought of how wrong she'd been about Kristy stealing her earrings all those years ago and how it had impacted the way she felt about her. She wasn't going to make the same mistake with Madison.

"All right," Janet said. "If you're good with hiring her, so am I."

"Great. I'll tell Madison to come in on Saturday for training."

"Will you ask your mom to help too?"

"I'm not sure," Debbie said. "Maybe I'll spend some time right now getting Madison acquainted with where everything is. We can start her busing tables and delivering orders."

"That sounds good. I'll come in earlier Saturday morning and make more doughnuts since we ran out last Saturday."

"I will too," Debbie said. "We'll make it work."

Madison grinned broadly when Debbie told her she had the job. "It won't be many hours," Debbie added. "Just a few a week, at the most. Some weeks there won't be any."

"I don't care." Madison grinned.

Debbie smiled in return. Madison was a go-getter. "Do you have time for me to show you around the kitchen and storeroom? We can also discuss what our expectations would be, along with filling out paperwork. That way, when you come in on Saturday, we can concentrate on your tasks for the day. I'll pay you for your time now, of course."

"Yes." Madison slid off the stool and grabbed her latte. "I'm so excited. Wait until I tell Jaxon."

Debbie gave her a questioning look.

"We're just friends," Madison quickly added. "But he's a cool guy."

Debbie agreed. As she led the way to the kitchen, she thought of the night the model depot went missing. "Did you go to volleyball practice the afternoon of homecoming?"

"No," Madison said. "Our coach knew everyone would be getting ready for the dance, so she gave us the afternoon off."

"So you didn't have your volleyball bag with you at the depot?"

Madison shook her head. "No." She looked closely at Debbie and then rolled her eyes. "Did you think, all this time, that I hid the model depot in my volleyball bag?"

Debbie wrinkled her nose.

Madison crossed her arms.

"I did think it could be a possibility."

"Well, now you know it wasn't."

"Now I know." Debbie continued to the kitchen, completely crossing Madison off her mental list of suspects. That left Jaxon and Kristy as the top contenders. And Dylan. He was the only one besides Madison who had been in the museum the night the depot was stolen *and* at Good Shepherd the day the painting went missing. Although Ian was right. No one had come up with a motive for Dylan.

It was time to ask some more questions about that young man. And she knew just where to start.

CHAPTER SEVENTEEN

The next afternoon after Debbie closed the café, she walked home with a box of a dozen cookies from Saturday that hadn't sold. Debbie contemplated taking the cookies by Kristy and Carson's but decided against it. She hadn't called Kristy as she'd planned, but she'd do it when she reached her house. It would be better to set up a time for them to meet rather than popping by.

She could take the cookies to Good Shepherd for Eileen and Ray to share, but it could be Ray's last evening with Gayle. She'd take the cookies tomorrow.

As she reached her front door, her phone rang. *Ray.* "Hello," she said in her cheeriest voice. "How are you?"

"A little down," Ray said. "Trudy ended up taking Gayle home this afternoon. I miss her already."

"Of course you do." She balanced the cookies in one hand and unlocked the door.

"Even at ninety-one, she's still my little sister," Ray said. "I wish I could have protected her that night."

"You took good care of her after the accident," Debbie said. "And all through the week."

"Thanks." He sighed. "I wondered if I could speak with you about a couple of things in person. Would you like to come for dinner? It's fried chicken tonight with apple crisp for dessert."

The food at Good Shepherd was surprisingly good. Dad had insisted on it as director, saying it was one of the main pleasures for the residents. "I'd like that," Debbie said. "I'll be there in about a half hour." She'd take the cookies with her.

When she arrived, she signed in as usual. This time Ashley was at her desk, typing away. "How's it going?" Debbie asked her.

"Good. Finally getting the hang of things around here. Anything I can do to help you?"

"Yes," Debbie answered, taking her wallet out of her purse. "I'd like to pay for dinner tonight."

Ashley stood and took Debbie's card, ran it, and then gave her a receipt. "Show this to your waiter."

Debbie took the receipt and tucked it into her wallet. "There's one more thing you can help me with."

Ashley smiled. "Anything."

"What is your impression of Dylan Rhodes, the boy who volunteers here?"

"Oh, he seems like a nice young man. Super courteous. Good with the residents. Always on time."

"What does he do?"

"We have two women who are blind. He reads to them."

Debbie's heart warmed. That was sweet. "Has he been coming this week?"

"Yes. Like clockwork."

"So you haven't had any trouble with him?" Debbie lowered her voice. "Nothing's gone missing?"

Ashley leaned forward and lowered her voice. "Like Ray's painting?"

Debbie nodded.

Ashley sat up straight. "No one's reported anything else missing. The daughter of one of the women he reads to comes in at least once a week and does an inventory of the items in her mother's room. She's never reported anything missing."

"Thank you." As Debbie headed down the hall with the box of cookies, she remembered she hadn't called Kristy as she meant to. She'd do it when she got home. It wouldn't be too late.

When she reached the sitting area, Kim called out, "Hello, Debbie!" She was sitting next to her mother on the couch, and Sofia sat on the other side of Eileen.

"Hello!" Debbie responded. "So nice to see the three of you."

"Are you here to see Ray?" Eileen asked.

"Yes. I'm going to have dinner with him."

Eileen said, "I'm glad you're here. He's a little down with Gayle leaving."

"He sounded sad on the phone," Debbie said. It was unlike him not to be in the sitting area, especially if Eileen was out of her room. Debbie put the cookies on the table. "I brought pumpkin sugar cookies from Saturday, although I heard there's apple crisp for dessert."

"Well, we'll just have to have our first dessert in the dining hall and then our second dessert back here." Eileen stood and gestured toward Ray's door. "Join us in the dining hall when he's ready. We'll save you seats."

Debbie knocked on Ray's door and then knocked again.

Finally, he called out, "Coming." When he opened the door, he blinked a couple of times, appearing a little bleary-eyed.

"Come in," he said. "I must have dozed off while I was waiting for you." He turned toward the closet. "I just need to get my sweater."

"Eileen, Kim, and Sofia are saving us seats at their table. I hope that's all right."

"Of course…" Ray's voice trailed off as he pulled a navy blue sweater from a hanger.

Debbie stepped forward and took his sweater from him. She held it so it would be easier for him to slip into. "How was Gayle today?"

"Good," he said. "Remarkable, actually. She's really bounced back."

"Is there anything you want to talk with me about before we join the others?"

"Yes," he said. "Eileen knows this, but Kim and Sofia don't need to be bored by the details of the accident. Gayle's insurance company, based on Ian's report, determined that the accident was Dylan's fault."

"That's good to hear."

He nodded. "Now that Gayle is on the mend and the insurance process is beginning, I've been thinking about my painting more." He met Debbie's gaze. "Any more information on it? Or the model depot?"

Debbie shook her head. "I'm afraid not."

"I woke up during the night thinking about both. What do you think happened?"

"I don't know," Debbie answered. "But I still think we'll find them."

"I hope so." Ray wheeled toward the door. "Let's go eat."

Once they were seated at the table and Debbie, Kim, and Sofia had shown their receipts, the waiter brought out beverages and green salads. After saying grace, Ray gave Kim and Sofia an update on Gayle.

Sofia dabbed at the edges of her mouth with her napkin. "Would you let me know the next time Gayle is in town? I have such fond memories of her as a child. I'd love to see her."

"Yes," Ray said. "She'd like that. She shared some memories of you from when you were little."

Sofia blushed.

Ray glanced at Debbie. "Gayle asked me to tell you that she remembered Anna's maiden name. It came to her in the middle of the night. It was Barrett."

"Thank you," Debbie said.

"I doubt it will help any," Ray said.

"You never know," Debbie said. "I think it's definitely worth researching what happened to her."

"Have you found the gold coins?" Ray asked Sofia, changing the subject.

Sofia shook her head. "I've searched the house, including the attic and the basement. Now I'm looking through Daddy's work area, although I doubt they're there. If Mama hadn't mentioned them in the letter, I wouldn't believe they existed. Honestly, I'm still having a difficult time believing they exist, regardless."

"I heard rumors that your mother brought a treasure with her from France." Ray smiled at Sofia. "But I think both your parents would have said you were the treasure your mother brought with her."

Sofia smiled back. "Why thank you, Ray. That will be my consolation if I never find the gold coins."

"How heavy would that have been to carry?" Kim asked. "Would it have been too heavy for Marguerite?"

Eileen turned to Sofia. "I was at the station when you arrived."

"What?"

"Remember, I was the stationmaster then. And Bob had been talking about you and your mother for weeks. I knew you were coming from Chicago—your father told me every day—so I made sure to be on the platform that day. Your mother had a small trunk with her."

Sofia folded her hands on top of the table. "Do you remember what we looked like?"

"I'll never forget." Eileen smiled. "You were both tiny and underfed. You both stayed small but, thankfully, after a few months, you didn't appear to be malnourished. You wore a cute little sailor dress with black patent leather shoes, and your mother wore a pleated black skirt, an ivory jacket, and a black hat. I doubt anyone that stylish had ever stepped off a train in Dennison. With all the shortages going on, and even more so in Europe, I have no idea how she managed to pull that off."

"I remember that skirt, jacket, and hat of Mama's," Sofia said. "But from when I was older."

"Yes, she paired those items with other garments for years. She made everything last."

"How did they get the trunk home?"

"Your father drove to the depot. He had an old pickup he used for his carpentry business."

Sofia grinned. "I remember his pickup. I was so sad when he got a new one. I was in high school by then."

"Have you found a trunk in your search for the coins?" Debbie asked.

"I have, in the attic," Sofia answered. "But it was empty."

Eileen put her fork down. "Have you found any odd keys?"

"No. I've confirmed that at one time Mama did have a safe-deposit box at the bank, but she closed it in 1973."

"Interesting," Eileen said.

"I graduated from college the year before and was teaching at Claymont High School. Perhaps she'd saved the coins as a safety net for me and then sold them when she saw I could support myself."

"She implied once that her family had been wealthy," Eileen said. "Do you think the coins were from your maternal grandparents?"

"I have no idea," Sofia said. "I asked her over and over for information about them, and she always said vague things, like they 'lived outside of Marseilles' and she hadn't seen them 'since before the war began.' When I went to Paris and Normandy as a college student, I asked her to let her relatives know I'd be in France. She said there were none left to see. I didn't believe her."

"She must have had her reasons," Eileen said.

"I'm sure she did. I've thought through it over and over. For as secretive as she was, you'd think her father was part of the Vichy government that cooperated with Germany or something."

When no one responded, Sofia said, "That's ludicrous, right?"

Eileen shrugged. "All sorts of strange things happened during the war."

"Well, I don't think it was anything like that," Sofia said. "I just keep thinking she would have left some sort of information for me. But I've nearly gone through the entire house now." She sighed. "It's amazing how much stuff we saved."

The waiter arrived with their chicken dinners on a large tray. Once each of them was served, Sofia said, "I have to remind myself that I had what mattered—a loving father and mother. And I guess if I truly wanted to find out about my French relatives, I would have taken a DNA test when they were first available instead of waiting until now. For some reason I felt getting one might hurt Mama's and Daddy's—more Mama's—feelings."

Debbie buttered her roll. "Speaking of your mother and father, any chance Anna Barrett is the person who confronted your family outside the movie theater all those years ago?"

"According to Gayle, she had a crush on your dad and never got over him marrying your mother," Ray added.

"How strange," Sofia said.

Ray glanced at Eileen. "Did you date Bob in high school?"

Eileen laughed. "No—although he was a good dancer." She grinned. "But we didn't date."

Sofia's eyes twinkled. "So you weren't jealous when Daddy married Mama?" she teased.

Eileen laughed again. "I couldn't have been happier for him."

"You must have been happy for him." Sofia cut her chicken. "Because you befriended Mama right away."

"Well, I *tried* to befriend your mother right away. It took a while, but I was persistent."

"What made you persistent?" Debbie dug into her mashed potatoes.

"That still, small voice." Eileen smiled. "That's when you know the nudge is from God. From the time I saw your mother on the depot platform in April of 1947, I wanted to be her friend. I invited her for coffee, but she politely declined. I invited her to Bible study, but she declined. It wasn't until I invited her to go on a picnic by the waterfall on the way to Bowerston that she accepted my invitation. We took the train and had a lovely day. After that, we were friends."

"Did I go with you?" Sofia asked.

"Yes," Eileen said. "You were four."

"It took over two years for Mama to accept an invitation from you?"

"Yes," Eileen answered. "After that we all went together to McCluskey Park. Then for walks along Little Stillwater Creek. Shopping downtown. I was open to whatever she wanted to do." Eileen had a faraway look in her eyes. "I think it was hard for her to know who she could trust. She mostly kept her business private, but I can see how Anna's behavior—along with others'—would have made her even more leery of developing friendships."

"Did you hear rumors about Mama?" Sofia asked.

Eileen nodded.

"Like what?"

"Oh, that she'd trapped your father. That she used him to get to America. None of it was true."

There was a long pause around the table.

"Tell me about your aunt Minnie," Debbie finally said to Sofia.

"Daddy's little sister?"

Debbie nodded and took a bite of her salad.

"She used to babysit me when I was little, but the older I got the less we saw her, until she was old and ill and moved in with Mama and Daddy. Sadly, I didn't know anything about my mother's family, and my father's family was distant." She wiped her mouth with her napkin. "Daddy used to say, 'We're not going to care what others think of us, because it's not our business to know. And if they choose to share what they think about us, we'll ignore them. Instead, we'll keep loving each other and our neighbors—which means everyone—as the good Lord commanded.'"

"That's really good advice," Debbie said.

"It is," Sofia said. "But it hurt to know people in town didn't accept us, including our own relatives."

CHAPTER EIGHTEEN

t was late by the time Debbie got to bed after getting caught up on laundry and housecleaning. Then she tossed and turned, thinking about Sofia. She'd started out wanting to find the model depot and then the painting—and she still did—but even more so she wanted to help Sofia uncover her story and find the gold coins, if they truly existed. The coins could make it possible for Sofia to keep the house, and information about her past could bring closure in her senior years. They had to find the depot.

Debbie continued to toss and turn some more, thinking about the earrings. What kind of teenager had she been, not being more aware of what was going on in Kristy's life and more empathetic overall?

Probably a normal teenager. One trying to figure out her identity and who she could trust to be loyal. She'd felt betrayed by Kristy all those years ago. But instead, she'd betrayed Kristy.

The next morning, Debbie stared at the earrings on the top of her dresser. She hadn't worn them yet. Would she? She slipped them into the pocket of her jeans. Perhaps she'd put them on once she reached the café.

An hour later, she shuffled into work, grateful for the scent of coffee that greeted her. Thankfully Janet had started a pot.

Janet stepped out of the kitchen. "You look exhausted."

"Thanks."

"I'm serious. Are you feeling all right?"

Debbie nodded. "I just had a rough night."

"Because?"

Debbie didn't answer as she put on her apron.

"What's going on?" Janet asked.

Debbie had waited longer than she should have to tell Janet about finding the earrings. "Remember those earrings you gave me that I thought Kristy stole the beginning of our junior year?"

Janet sighed. "Why are you bringing those up again? They probably got misplaced or something. You were always losing things."

Debbie's mouth dropped open. "I was not."

"You were. Your driver's license. Your retainer. Your backpack."

Debbie thought a moment. She had lost all of those at one time or another.

Janet sighed. "So what's making you bring up the earrings again?"

"Mom found a box in the back of the spare bedroom closet."

Janet leaned against the doorframe. "And the earrings were in it?"

"Yes." Debbie tied her apron a little tighter. "I think I need to talk to Kristy, but what if she doesn't remember?"

"Remember what?"

"That I asked her if she knew what happened to the earrings."

Janet's eyes grew large. "You mean if she remembers you accusing her of stealing the earrings."

"I didn't accuse her—"

Janet's eyebrows shot up. "You need to speak with her. I'll bet she remembers. Most teenage girls wouldn't forget that."

Debbie nodded. Janet was right. "I'll call her this morning and see if she can come in or if we can meet for a walk this evening."

"Good idea." Janet headed back into the kitchen.

"Wait," Debbie said. "We need to talk about Sofia."

Janet stopped and turned around.

"Would you have time soon to find out what happened to Anna Barrett?"

"I can do some research tomorrow," Janet said. "Hopefully Patricia will have some answers for us about Sofia's birth certificate. Any progress on who took the model depot and the painting?"

"No. I've ruled out Madison. So that leaves Dylan as a suspect in both the theft of the model depot as well as the painting, even though none of us can come up with a motive for him."

"And about the depot, is Kristy the main suspect?"

"After Dylan, yes," Debbie answered. "And Jaxon. And maybe Julian and Roger."

Janet laughed. "You think Roger Dunn took it?"

"He was in the parking lot hanging around at the end of the night."

Janet waved her hand. "That doesn't mean anything," she said. "Anyone else?"

Debbie shook her head. "I wonder if Kim has already commissioned a new depot."

"That would be a shame," Janet said. "Especially considering Bob Jennings made it and Marguerite painted it."

"I know." Debbie followed Janet into the kitchen. "I feel like I know both of them now, even though they're both gone."

Janet nodded. "Although, remember, I became acquainted with Marguerite at the bakery. Remember? I told you she loved my macarons."

"Wow. I wish she would have come into our café. But it doesn't sound as if she was mobile enough toward the end."

"She wasn't," Janet said. "She went downhill pretty fast."

An hour later, Patricia and Harry came in, right on time. As Harry sat down and Crosby settled at his feet, Patricia continued to the counter. "Debbie, I didn't find Sofia's original birth certificate, but I found some general information."

"Great. I'll get Janet. And I'll pour Harry a cup of coffee and make your mocha. Then we can talk."

A few minutes later, Patricia held her mocha while Debbie and Janet stood in front of her.

She took out her phone. "I emailed myself the document as a reminder. Because Bob Jennings served honorably..." She began to read: "'...in the US Armed Forces after December 7, 1941, and he was a citizen of the US, and because his child resided in the US for five years between the ages of thirteen and twenty-one, said child will acquire US citizenship.'" She looked up. "That's according to the Nationality Act of 1940."

"That's fascinating," Janet said. "Marguerite wouldn't take Sofia to France with her in the early 1960s, when Sofia would have been a teenager. I wonder if she was afraid of jeopardizing her US citizenship."

"That could be," Debbie added, "but Sofia thinks it was because of secrets her mother kept about her parents. Marguerite's father had passed away by then, but for some reason Marguerite refused to let Sofia know anything about her family."

"Maybe it was both," Patricia said. "Marguerite might have thought there was a chance she could end up staying in France longer than a year."

"My understanding is that Marguerite went thinking she'd stay until her mother passed away," Debbie said.

"Marguerite could have sent Sofia home after a few months, even a few weeks. It sounds as if she was hiding something." Janet addressed Patricia. "What about adoption records for Sofia? Were there any?"

"She needs to check. Ohio adoption records prior to 1964 can be accessed by an adoptee with the proper identification. There's a form online she can print out and mail in."

"I'll tell her," Debbie said. "She's expecting the results from a DNA test soon, so she'll probably wait to find out what it reveals. I think she'll want to see if there's any adoption information on her, to find out the truth."

"The absence of an adoption record doesn't mean she was Bob's biological daughter."

"What do you mean?"

"She might not have had a French birth certificate. If she did, the Ohio adoption records would include it. But Marguerite might not have been able to get a French birth certificate for Sofia. To get a US birth certificate once they were in the States, back then, all that would have been needed was Bob swearing he was her father."

"Interesting," Debbie said. "I'll give Sofia the information."

The morning progressed, and by ten the breakfast rush had ended. Debbie sat at the far table, intent on calling Kristy before Janet had to remind her. She pulled her phone from her apron pocket. She could text, but that seemed cowardly. She placed the call, which immediately went to voice mail.

Debbie hesitated. "Hi, Kristy. It's Debbie. I was hoping to speak with you sometime soon. Any chance you could stop by the café for your morning break? For a drink and pastry on me." She ended the call and headed back to the counter, to find Kristy sitting on a stool holding her phone.

"You called?"

Debbie managed a smile. "I did. Did you listen to my message yet?"

Kristy shook her head.

"I need to talk with you about something," Debbie explained. "I asked if you could take your morning break here. I said your drink and pastry would be on me."

"Sounds serious."

"It is." Debbie nodded toward the table in the far corner. "Let's sit over there."

Debbie made Kristy's drink—a pumpkin spice latte again—and plated an apple fritter and then joined her.

Kristy had a concerned expression on her face. "What's going on? Does this have to do with the missing model depot?"

"No." Debbie was tempted to ask, *Should it?* But she bit her tongue. She didn't want to falsely accuse Kristy a second time. "Do you remember our junior year, on my birthday, when the earrings Janet gave me went missing?"

Kristy leaned back in her chair. "And you accused me of taking them?"

"I think, if I remember right, I asked if you'd seen them."

Kristy paused a moment. "But you thought I took them, right?"

Debbie grimaced. "I did. And I'm so sorry for that. It was wrong of me."

Kristy tilted her head. "What brought this up?"

Debbie explained about the box. "The earrings were in it, jammed in a birthday card." She pulled the earrings from the pocket of her jeans. "Here they are. I really am sorry. For some reason I felt justified back then in asking if you knew where they were, but that was a mistake. I'm afraid it affected our friendship."

Kristy exhaled and blinked a few times. "I tried to forget about all that, especially after I found out you'd moved back to Dennison."

"You were so gracious to me," Debbie said. "Accepting Mom's invitation to Sunday dinner, inviting me to your house for dinner. Planning my birthday dinner at your house. You had every right to treat me poorly, and yet you didn't. Apologizing to me for being distant the last two years of high school—when I'd been the one who hurt you."

"You were a good friend except for that one incident. I wanted to be friends with you again. I wanted to put all that behind us and not hold it against you." Kristy paused a moment. "I chose to move forward."

"Well, thank you for being so gracious and forgiving, even before I asked for forgiveness. I really appreciate it."

Kristy reached across the table and squeezed Debbie's hand. "I'm glad you found the earrings."

"Thank you," Debbie said. "I'm sorry about your mother. I had no idea she was ill while we were in high school."

"Not many people did. She didn't want people feeling sorry for her..." Kristy's voice trailed off. "She lived with cancer for six years, so maybe she was right. There was no need to talk about it that early."

"I wish I'd known," Debbie said.

Kristy smiled. "I wish I'd told you. I needed more support, even if my mother felt she didn't. And it felt like such a heavy secret. There was no reason for her to require me to keep it like she did." Kristy took a sip of her latte and gazed out the window toward the train tracks. Then she looked at Debbie again. "You said I was gracious to you and a good friend. But you've been the same to me, and I appreciate it. Even though you most likely still thought I'd taken the earrings."

It was Debbie's turn to reach across the table and squeeze Kristy's hand.

Kristy dug into her apple fritter, and Debbie headed back to the kitchen. The encounter had gone much better than she anticipated.

But Kristy could be gracious about Debbie accusing her of stealing the earrings all those years ago *and* be the one who stole the model depot. The two weren't mutually exclusive. She slipped the earrings back into her pocket.

Maybe that was the reason Kristy had been so nice to Debbie since returning to Dennison. Maybe it was a cover for taking the depot.

Janet left at two, ready to go find out what had become of Anna Barrett. An hour later, after Debbie finished her closing tasks, she boxed up four leftover apple fritters for Ray to share. She grabbed forks and napkins, put everything in a bag, and then headed to her house for her car.

Ten minutes later, she walked down the hall toward Ray's apartment, but she stopped when she reached the sitting area. Carson sat on the sofa across from where Ray sat in his wheelchair, next to Eileen. All three appeared to be deep in conversation.

"Hello," Debbie said.

All three turned to her.

"Hi, Carson," Debbie said. "Did you meet your deadline?"

He stood. "Debbie, how nice to see you." He gave her a hug. "I hit send a minute before midnight. Now I'm working on my next article. I hope to compare the experience of someone who worked for the railroad in their hometown with someone who left that same hometown by rail for the war."

"Well, I can't think of any two people more perfect to interview than Eileen and Ray." Debbie held up the bag. "I brought apple fritters for an afternoon snack."

Carson stood. "I need to get going. It's time to start dinner." He picked up his tablet. "Thank you, Eileen and Ray." He stepped closer and shook Ray's hand. "I'll stop by if I have any follow-up questions."

After they all told Carson goodbye, Debbie held up the bag. "Ready for an apple fritter?"

Eileen stood. "Let's go to my room and sit at the table. It's easier to eat, and I'll make tea." She stood and put her hands on the back of Ray's chair. "Let's go."

Ray turned his head and smiled.

Eileen's room was filled with photographs—on the walls, end tables, and bookcases. She had many black-and-white photos, some over a hundred years old. And new photos, including a framed school photo of Madison. She even had a digital photo frame that displayed recent photos.

"Have a seat," Eileen said. "I'll get some plates and make the tea."

Debbie sat and took out the apple fritters. "I have forks and napkins," she said as Eileen put three plates on the table.

After the tea had brewed, Eileen served it and then sat down. "After our discussion yesterday," she said, "I did a little research on World War II war brides on my desktop and printed out some information."

"Nice," Debbie said. "I didn't realize you had a computer here."

"Oh, yes. It's on my desk in my bedroom. I use it for email, social media, and research. I'm trying to write up my memories for Madison. I work on that for an hour every morning."

Debbie sighed. "That's wonderful. What a gift." She wished one of her grandparents had done that for her.

"I'll get my notes from my research." Eileen set her fork on her plate. "Excuse me."

Ray swallowed his first bite of apple fritter and said, "Janet outdid herself on this one."

"I agree." She took a bite and then a sip of tea as Eileen returned with a notebook and her reading glasses.

She sat down, pushed her plate toward the middle of the table, and placed the notebook in front of her. Then she perched her reading glasses on her nose. "It's all quite fascinating. If I ever knew any of this, I forgot." The page in front of her was filled with notes, many of them bulleted. "'Sixty to seventy thousand women married American servicemen during World War II and hoped to leave their countries behind and join their husbands for a new life in the US. However, restrictive American immigration polices, such as the Immigration Act of 1924, which was a quota system, created challenges.'" She paused and ran her finger to the next line. "'The War Brides Act, enacted on December 28, 1945, was created to expedite the admission to the United States of alien spouses and alien minor children of citizen members of the United States armed forces. They were known as 'war brides,' and their dependents were exempted from the quota systems and granted free passage to journey to their new homes.'"

She continued, "'Far more than the expected number arrived. The subsequent Alien Fiancées and Fiancés Act of 1946 and 1947 increased the numbers to nearly 300,000 women and dependents, who made their way to the United States before the expiration of the War Brides Act and similar acts in December 1948.'" She took her reading glasses off. "Marguerite and Sofia weren't alone, and yet they were very alone here in Dennison."

Debbie agreed. "Even as a girl, over forty years after they arrived, I remember being told by other kids that Marguerite was a war bride and Sofia was a war child. I only remember seeing them downtown and being fascinated by them."

"Those terms were probably passed down from generation to generation," Eileen said. "I think of all the things Marguerite contributed to our community—her painting and food and gardening come to mind first. But there was so much more she could have given us. Her stories of the war. Her language. Her culture. On the one hand, I think she felt safe and cared for here, mostly because of Bob. But, on the other hand, I fear she never felt she could truly be herself."

"That's sad," Debbie said as she picked up her mug.

"And I'm afraid all of that encouraged her to keep secrets from Sofia," Eileen said. "I think she believed she was protecting Sofia, when in fact she was withholding important information from her."

Debbie set her cup down. "Such as?"

"Well, I've wondered over the years if Bob was her biological father." Eileen cut another bite of her fritter. "I never would have said anything if Sofia hadn't started questioning it herself. She was an absolute mini-me of Marguerite, which might have meant nothing. Bob was blond and blue-eyed, and if I remember correctly from biology class all those years ago, those genes are recessive." She sighed. "This is going to sound odd, but Bob wasn't a normal parent back then. He was so intentional about his parenting, so thoughtful. In some ways he treated Sofia as a princess, but it wasn't just that. It seemed as if he was trying to make up for something. For some sort of loss." She shrugged. "I may have imagined all of that though. Or maybe he was compensating for his lost time with Sofia as a baby."

"Interesting," Debbie said. "You don't think Marguerite would have told Sofia if it was true?"

"I would like to hope Marguerite would have, but it wouldn't surprise me…" Eileen's voice trailed off. "Maybe there's still a letter or a tape recording or something. That wouldn't be as good as Marguerite telling her in person, but it would be better than nothing, if it was true. Then again, I could be completely wrong about the whole thing."

Eileen began eating her apple fritter.

"How did you become acquainted with Carson, Ray?" Debbie asked.

"Oh, Kim recommended he talk with Eileen and me about what the railroad was like here during the war."

"So you met him today?"

"No, I met him last week. Eileen was busy, though, the day he came by."

"That's right," Eileen said. "I was doing Madison's class."

"Carson came by to introduce himself and set up a time we could talk. He wants to do it this week since he has a deadline on Monday. Nice guy."

Debbie leaned forward. "Where did you talk with him last week?"

"In my apartment. Madison led the exercise class out in the sitting area." Ray picked up his mug. "His wife was with him. Nice gal. Her name is…" He shook his head.

"Kristy," Debbie said.

Ray nodded. "Yes, her name is Kristy."

"So she was in your apartment too? The day the painting went missing?"

Ray put his mug back down without taking a drink. "I think they were here before the painting went missing. I didn't notice it was gone until after dinner."

"Did they have any bags with them?"

Ray thought for a moment. "Well, yes. They both did. She had a big purse, and he had a backpack. Why? What are you thinking?"

"I hate to unjustly accuse anyone, but we might need to consider that one of them could have taken it," Debbie said.

Or both. Maybe they were working together.

CHAPTER NINETEEN

When Debbie reached the lobby of Good Shepherd and stopped at the counter to sign out, she scanned the sheet, looking for Carson's name. It wasn't there.

"Hi, Debbie." Ashley came from the direction of the dining hall. "How are you?"

"Good. Hey, do you have the sign-in sheet from a week ago Monday?" Debbie thought a minute. "It would have been the ninth."

"Sure. I have it right here." Ashley stepped behind the counter to the desk. She pulled a file from the bottom drawer and returned to the counter, thumbing through the file as she did. "Here it is." She placed the sign-in sheet in front of Debbie.

Debbie skimmed it. It was as she remembered it. Madison and Dylan signed in at one fifteen, and she herself had signed in at seven fifteen, but Carson hadn't signed in at all. "Can I look at the sign-in sheet for the tenth, please?" Perhaps Ray had mixed up the days.

"Here it is."

Carson's name wasn't on that one either. Debbie handed both sheets back to Ashley.

Ashley returned them to the file. "Unfortunately, not everyone signs in. If I'm at my desk or at the counter, I insist. But if I'm somewhere else in the building, sometimes people waltz right by the sign-in sheet. Visitors. Volunteers. Vendors. I don't get it. Don't they want to keep our residents safe?"

"Most people probably don't realize how important it is, or even that it's here."

"I appreciate that you take the time to do it," Ashley said. "You know it's important."

Debbie nodded. She wanted nothing more than to keep the senior citizens of Dennison safe. After telling Ashley goodbye, Debbie stopped before the exit and sent a text to Ian about Carson and Kristy both being in Ray's room the afternoon the painting was stolen. Then she put her phone in her pocket and stepped out into a drizzling rain. She paused at the ding of her phone. Expecting it to be Ian, she pulled it from her jacket pocket. A text from Janet. I FOUND SOME INFO ABOUT ANNA BARRETT. WANT TO STOP BY? IAN'S WORKING LATE.

SURE. LEAVING GOOD SHEPHERD. BE THERE SOON.

When Debbie arrived at Janet's she knocked once and then opened the door. "Honey, I'm home!" she called out and then stopped in the entryway and took a deep breath, filling her lungs with the savory scent of beef. What was Janet cooking?

"In the kitchen," Janet called.

Of course Janet was in the kitchen. It astounded Debbie that her friend could cook all day at the café and then go home and cook some more. As Debbie stepped into the kitchen, Janet waved from where she stirred a pot on the stove.

"Whatcha makin'?" Debbie asked.

"Beef Stroganoff. Want some?"

"Of course."

Janet took a bowl from the cupboard, filled it with egg noodles, and then ladled the beef Stroganoff over the top. She put it on the counter and grabbed another bowl. "There's sparkling water in the fridge."

"Sounds good. Do you want one too?"

"Please," Janet said.

Debbie poured the drinks, and then she and Janet sat down at the table. "Thank you," Debbie said. "I probably would have had toast for dinner."

Janet made a face. "You can cook."

Debbie made a face back. It wasn't that she couldn't cook. "Sometimes I enjoy cooking for just myself, but other times it seems like the biggest chore in the world."

Janet said a blessing for the food, and then Debbie took a bite. "Oh my goodness." She held her fork in midair. "This is delicious. Can we make it for the café?"

Janet laughed. "I don't think we'd have enough interest."

"I know our customers would love this."

"We're not really that sort of café. This is more like diner food."

"We could be." Debbie took another bite. "This is the best."

"I'll give you the recipe." Janet tasted the dish and cocked her head. "It needs more mustard."

"Mustard?" Debbie didn't taste mustard at all.

"Grey Poupon."

Debbie laughed. "I should have guessed." She ate another forkful. "I have a quick update. Both Carson and Kristy were at Good Shepherd, in Ray's room, the day the painting was stolen."

"Yikes," Janet said. "Did you tell Ian?"

"I sent him a text but haven't heard back from him yet."

"So with this new information, have you crossed Dylan off the list?"

"I think so," Debbie answered. "No motive plus no evidence equals no suspect, right?"

Janet nodded.

Debbie sipped her water . "What did you find out about Anna?"

"Well, Anna was married twice, the second time to Mike Roth in 1962. They had one child. But before that she was married to Stephen Jennings."

Debbie choked. "Jennings?"

"Yes."

"Any relation to Bob Jennings?"

Janet gave Debbie a sassy look. "I'm glad you asked. Yes. Stephen and Bob were first cousins."

"You're kidding."

"No. I'm serious."

"What year did Anna and Stephen get married?"

"1949."

"Any children?"

"Yes, two girls. One, Esther, in 1950, and the other, Priscilla, in 1955."

Debbie leaned across the table. "Esther? That's the name of the woman you talked to at the library."

"Exactly."

Debbie leaned back in her chair. "But why would she tell you Sofia was adopted?"

"I don't know, but I have two guesses. Either she's picked up her mother's grudge and wants to keep the rumor going that Sofia was adopted, or else she thinks Sofia should finally know the truth."

As Debbie climbed the steps at home to head to bed, Greg texted. Several times today I intended to call but kept getting distracted. Work. Picking the boys up from practice. Dinner. Homework. And here it is, almost 11. How was your day?

She reached her room and sat down on the bed. Good. Yours?

Busy, LOL. Want to go to Jaxon's football game tomorrow? Starts at 5. At Dennison Stadium.

I'd love that, Debbie texted back. See you there.

He sent her a thumbs-up emoji.

She put her phone on her nightstand, crawled into bed, and pulled the covers to her chin. Given the discovery at Good Shepherd that both Kristy and Carson had been in Ray's apartment the day his painting went missing, they were now the top two suspects. And to think they were hosting her birthday dinner in two days. Well, if she could prove they worked together to take the model depot and the painting, or prove that one of them did, Mom and Dad could always host her birthday party.

What would inspire Carson to take the items? Was it more than his interest in the railways and the Dennison Depot in particular? Ray had wanted to collect depot items but hadn't found enough of them to make a collection. Perhaps Carson had.

Then again, Debbie hadn't ruled out Jaxon. Just because Carson and Kristy had the opportunity to take both the depot and the painting, it didn't mean they did. If Jaxon took the depot, he was probably too embarrassed to return it now.

But what about the painting? A wandering resident could have taken it. It might still show up.

Debbie burrowed her head into her feather pillow. She said a prayer, asking God for guidance when it came to finding the depot and the painting and then asking Him to reveal the truth of the past to Sofia, in all things.

The next morning, a little after ten, Sofia came into the café with a faded green portfolio.

Debbie greeted her at the counter.

"I'll just have coffee," Sofia said. "And I was hoping I could show you something. Do you have a minute?"

"Yes," Debbie said. "Hold on a second." She poured the coffee, told Janet she was taking a few minutes to speak with a customer, and then joined Sofia at a table.

Sofia pushed her coffee cup to the middle of the table and opened the portfolio.

"What do you have?" Debbie asked as she sat down.

"Drawings. Ones I've never seen before."

"Wow." Debbie leaned forward as Sofia turned the top drawing toward her. The paper had yellowed, but the graphite had survived the years. The drawing was of a young woman sitting at a window. In the reflection of the glass was a young man, the artist.

"Look at the next one," Sofia said.

It was of the same couple except, this time, the young man was sitting at the window and the woman, who was now the artist, was the one reflected in the glass.

"Do you recognize either of the models?" Debbie asked.

"The woman is Mama," Sofia answered. "I have no idea who the man is. Perhaps a fellow student."

The next drawing was a disproportionate cityscape of Paris. In the center was the Place de la Concorde, with the Eiffel Tower and the Arc de Triomphe to the left. To the right were the Louvre and Notre-Dame. The Seine curved through the cityscape. The landmarks were all five times bigger than any of the other buildings in the drawing. Debbie squinted. "What's in the river?" Her eyes moved to the sky. "And the clouds?"

"Symbols," Sofia said. "Paintbrushes. Palettes. Letters. Perhaps some sort of code." She pointed out the objects. "I've studied this with a magnifying glass." She pointed again, this time to a cloud above Notre-Dame. "Coins." She pointed to the river below the Louvre. "And a key. And a mirror."

Alarmed, Debbie met Sofia's gaze. "Do you think your mother drew this?"

"I think whoever drew this also created the painting Ray had—or else someone who knew the drawing well. Perhaps it was my mother. Or someone she knew and emulated." She turned the drawing over onto the pile with the drawings of the two artists, revealing the drawing of a baby who appeared to be a year old or so and wore a smocked dress.

"Oh," Debbie said. "This is precious."

"It's me," Sofia said. "It's a drawing of the one baby picture I have of myself while we were still in France." She opened her purse and took out a photo. It was of herself, being held by a young woman who looked like the woman in the drawing but older—and tired. Both wore coats. The woman had a pillbox hat on her head, and the baby wore a bonnet.

"Mama told me I was eighteen months old when this picture was taken, six months before we left for the US."

"Did she draw pictures of you when you were older?"

Sofia thought for a moment. "No."

Sofia put the photograph back in her purse and turned the drawing of the baby over. It was the last drawing in the portfolio.

"What do you think all of this means?" Debbie asked.

"I have no idea. I'm happy to have these drawings. I'm going to get all four of them framed. But I wish, instead of leaving unexplained clues or whatever they are, Mama would have just talked to me and told me her secrets."

Debbie agreed. Sofia deserved to know her own story, even if she'd never entirely know her mother's.

After shopping for supplies for the weekend and returning to the café to put them all away, Debbie arrived at the Dennison Stadium at five minutes to five. She stood at the bottom of the stands for a moment, looking for Greg. She saw Julian first, jumping up and down and waving at her. Greg sat next to him, a smile on his face. He waved when she saw him.

Debbie waved back and started up the bleachers. "Hey," she said as she reached them. "How are you two doing?"

"Great." Greg stood and gave her a quick hug. "I stopped by Carson and Kristy's today to take a look at their kitchen. I already RSVP'd for your birthday dinner."

"Is Jaxon playing in the varsity game tomorrow night?" Debbie asked. "Because you don't have to come. I totally understand."

"He's going to suit up, but it's an away game at Sandy Valley. He most likely won't play."

Julian leaned forward. "I'm going to go to the game with Monty and his family. He's not here now because his mom—stepmom— took him to his orthodontist appointment and his dad is out of town on business. Brent is going to suit up for the game too."

"Nice," Debbie said. "That sounds like fun." She turned to Greg. "I don't want you to miss the game…"

She thought she'd spoken quietly enough that Julian hadn't heard, but he said, "Like Dad said, Jaxon isn't going to play. Dad won't be missing anything."

Greg grinned. "See? I'm looking forward to the party. Carson has all sorts of ideas for their kitchen remodel. And Kristy has ideas about other rooms in the house. Bookcases in her office, for example. She gave me a tour of the place."

Debbie grinned. "I'm jealous you got to see her backyard office."

Greg shook his head. "Her office is on the first floor, in one of the bedrooms. Carson uses the building in the backyard."

"Oh, I thought that was Kristy's space," Debbie said. "Maybe I just assumed that."

"Yeah, she said it was his playhouse as a kid. He had it fixed up before they moved in—wired, plumbed, and insulated. She said he's really found his muse since they moved back."

"Interesting…"

"Oh, and why didn't you tell me the model depot was found?"

Debbie's mouth dropped open. "It's been found?"

"That's what Kristy said."

Julian jumped to his feet. "That's great!"

"Weird." Why wouldn't Kim have told Debbie if that was true? "I hadn't heard."

Debbie waited until after the kickoff to text Kim. Just heard the model depot was found. That's great! Where was it?

She waited and waited. Finally, right before the end of the first half, Kim texted back. Where did you hear that? If it's been found, no one let me know. One of the railroad volunteers said he would make a new one.

As the team ran off the field, Debbie nudged Greg and showed him Kim's text. "Kim said the model depot hasn't been found."

He read the text. "Maybe I misunderstood Kristy."

Julian sighed and then stood. "I'm going to go play catch with the other guys on the field." A small crowd of middle-school students had already gathered. He raced down the bleachers, stumbling just before the bottom. Debbie gasped, but he caught himself and continued to the field.

"He's been restless—hyper—the last couple of days. And Jaxon's still been moody. I don't know what's going on." Greg looked at Debbie and sighed. "Sorry I didn't text or call for a couple of days.

It's been one of those weeks trying to get Julian to calm down and Jaxon to speak up."

"I'm sorry," Debbie said.

Greg shrugged. "I just wish I could read their minds."

She smiled. "I'm sure all parents feel that way sometimes."

"Probably."

When the game resumed, Jaxon started on the line as the Mustangs kicked off to the opposing team. Then he stayed in as a defensive end.

"They're short a couple of players today," Greg said. "Jaxon thought maybe he'd play some defense too."

Julian, who'd been standing on the sidelines, ran back up the bleachers as quickly as he ran down them, stumbling again near the middle and then, just as he reached them, slamming into Greg's shoulder.

"Bud, take it easy," Greg said. "I need that shoulder."

"Sorry." Julian sprawled out on the bench next to Greg.

"What's going on?"

Julian sat up and glanced at Debbie. "I was so excited to hear the depot was found—and then so bummed to find out it wasn't."

"Why?"

His voice dropped to a whisper, but Debbie could still hear him. "Jaxon took it."

Debbie froze while Greg blurted out, "What?"

"He took it to impress Madison," Julian said. "He has a huge crush on her."

Greg took off his baseball cap and ran his hand through his hair.

Debbie leaned forward. "Julian, did you see Jaxon take the model depot?"

Julian shook his head. "But he could have, easy."

"Have you seen the model depot at home?" Greg asked.

He shook his head again. "Jaxon gave the depot to Madison that night. I think he snuck out of the house."

"You *think*?" Greg asked. "These are serious accusations, Julian."

"He slept in my room that night. I woke up around midnight, and he wasn't there. When I woke up in the morning, he was." Julian began tapping his foot. "Don't tell Jaxon I said anything."

"Well, if he did take it, I do need to say something, but—" Greg stopped as the crowd began to cheer.

A pass from the other team went wide. Jaxon ran after it, his arms in the air. The ball sailed into his hands.

Both Greg and Julian leaped to their feet, and Greg yelled, "Way to go, Jax!"

Debbie stood, clapping.

Jaxon darted between two players on the opposing team and then rushed forward. He was forty yards from the end zone. He sped up, darting by another defender. And then another. Past that, he was free and practically floated to a touchdown.

Greg high-fived Julian and then Debbie. Julian jumped up and down and spun around. Jaxon, before being swarmed by his teammates, turned toward the stands, searching out Greg, who gave his son a thumbs-up.

Tears stung Debbie's eyes.

As Jaxon's teammates reached him, Greg said, "I'm going to take the boys out for pizza after the game. Would you come with us?"

"Yes."

"Would you help me bring up the subject of the model depot with Jaxon?" Greg asked. "If he did take it, I need to know that now and deal with it."

Debbie nodded. "I'll do my best."

CHAPTER TWENTY

The Mustangs won, 7-0, thanks to Jaxon's touchdown. On the way to the restaurant, the boys were jubilant in the back seat of Greg's extended-cab truck, reliving the interception and forty-yard run.

"Thank you for coming with us," Greg said.

"I'm happy to," Debbie replied and then silently said a prayer for help when they talked with Jaxon about the model depot. If he'd given it to Madison, she'd done a remarkable job hiding it and denying she had it.

When they reached Buona Vita, the boys tumbled out of the truck and dashed toward the front door.

Greg turned off the engine. "Should I say something about the missing depot now or wait?"

"I have a question for you before I answer. Was Carson in the room when Kristy said the model depot had been found?"

"No," Greg answered.

"Do you think you misunderstood Kristy?"

Greg thought for a moment and then said, "No. What are you getting at?"

She told him about both Carson and Kristy being at Good Shepherd the Monday Ray's painting went missing.

Greg considered that. "Do you think they took it?"

"I don't know," Debbie said. "But I'm wondering if we've missed something from the night of the alumni event."

"Well, I'd like to believe that anyone but Jaxon took the model depot," Greg said, "but I don't want to be in denial if Julian has a good reason to believe he did. It wasn't in his football bag, and I couldn't find it anywhere else in the house. But it could be tucked away in a box in the attic. Houses have a lot of hidey-holes, and kids seem to find them all."

Debbie agreed. She'd certainly had a few hiding places as a child.

"Do you want me to ask them exactly what they saw that night?" It bothered Debbie that Kristy had told Greg the depot had been found. Either she made that up, or Carson had told her that. Perhaps it was a misunderstanding, or perhaps one of them was trying to get a rumor started.

"Sure," Greg said. "I'll ask more questions depending on what his response is."

"How about if I text Kristy and ask where she heard the depot had been found? Is that all right with you?"

"Good idea," Greg said.

Debbie quickly sent the text, without saying Kim had told her that the model depot was still missing.

Kristy texted her back immediately. CARSON HEARD THAT FROM ANOTHER DOCENT AT THE MUSEUM. ISN'T THAT GREAT NEWS? THE OTHER DOCENT DIDN'T KNOW WHERE IT WAS FOUND. CARSON'S GOING TO TEXT KIM AND ASK HER.

Once they'd ordered their drinks and pizza and settled down at their table, Debbie's phone dinged again. Kristy. OOPS, FALSE

ALARM. THE DEPOT HASN'T BEEN FOUND. SORRY. THE OTHER VOLUNTEER MISUNDERSTOOD KIM.

Debbie showed the text to Greg without saying anything. He wrinkled his nose.

"What's going on?" Jaxon asked.

"There's a rumor going around that the model depot was found," Debbie told him, "but it wasn't. It would be helpful to an older woman named Sofia Jennings if we could find it—there may be something in the depot that her mother hid years ago." Jaxon and Julian looked at each other, their expressions full of annoyance. Debbie continued anyway. "Whether the hidden object is there or not, knowing one way or the other would be helpful to Sofia."

"You should tell Debbie the truth," Jaxon said to Julian.

Julian shook his head dramatically. "No, you should."

"What's going on?" Greg asked.

In unison, Jaxon and Julian pointed at the other and said, "He took the depot."

Debbie leaned back in her chair as Greg leaned forward, but before he could speak, Jaxon said, "I'm sorry. I shouldn't have protected Julian. It was wrong."

"Protected me? I was protecting you! It was stupid of you to take it to impress Madison."

Jaxon's face reddened. "I didn't take it. And I wouldn't try to impress Madison."

Julian blurted out, "You have a crush on her."

Jaxon crossed his arms. "No I don't." He lowered his voice. "Not anymore."

Debbie's heart lurched. These were good kids.

"Do either of you have any actual evidence the other took it?" Greg asked. "Did you witness the act? See the depot in the other's possession? See the depot hidden somewhere in the house? Witness it being given to Madison?"

Both boys shook their heads.

"I just figured Julian did, because Madison said she wanted it for her dad," Jaxon said. "I know I didn't do it."

Julian hung his head. "Same."

"I believe you both," Greg said, "but I'm sorry each of you thought the other took it. Next time, don't make assumptions. You need to have evidence before accusing someone."

Jaxon looked at Debbie. "Do you believe neither of us took it?"

"Absolutely," Debbie said. "But I'm thinking maybe you can still help us find it. Did you see anything odd that night that you've remembered? Or didn't tell us before?"

Jaxon's face grew red, and he dropped his head.

Greg said, "Jax…"

Jaxon exhaled and then said, "I saw a guy prop the back door open with something. I figured he needed to carry something out, but after the model went missing, well, it could have something to do with that."

"Why didn't you say anything before?" Greg asked.

Jaxon's face grew redder. "I don't know. By the time I remembered it, I thought maybe you wouldn't believe me or I might get blamed for not telling someone about it right away."

"Thank you for telling us now," Debbie said. "What did the guy look like?"

Jaxon's voice grew even fainter. "Probably about the same age as you guys. Dark hair with gray here." He touched his temples. "He was wearing a jacket. It was the first time I've ever seen him."

Debbie dropped her voice. "Have you seen him anywhere else since then?"

Jaxon nodded. "At my football game last week. Standing with you and Dad."

It was nine o'clock by the time Debbie walked into her house, both exhilarated and weary. It appeared she was closer to finding the thief. All the evidence pointed at Carson. Or Kristy. Or both.

No doubt, the birthday party the next day would be awkward.

She took off her shoes and slid her feet into her slippers. As she shuffled toward the kitchen to make a cup of tea, her phone rang.

Sofia. After greeting her, Sofia said, "I know it's late, but do you mind coming over? Kim is on her way, but I'd like you to be here too."

"Sure. What's up?"

"I found some things in the basement, in the storage room bookcase. More clues…"

"Yes." Debbie turned around. "It'll only take me a few minutes." She quickly put on her shoes and jacket and headed back into the crisp autumn night.

When she arrived at Sofia's, Kim was knocking on the door. "Hello!" Debbie called out and hurried up the porch stairs, her heartbeat accelerated by the brisk walk and anticipation of what Sofia had found.

"Hello," Kim said to Debbie as Sofia opened the door. Sofia's hair was twisted into a bun at the nape of her neck, and she wore an apron over a blouse and skirt.

"Thank you so much for coming," she said. "Please come in."

Kim led the way, and Debbie followed.

"I've made some tea," Sofia said. "And one of Mama's galette des rois, even though it's not Christmas. I've been thinking about her so much today, and baking one of her specialties helps me grieve."

She led them to the living room. A tray with a teapot, three cups, three plates, a knife, and a platter with the cake sat in the middle of the coffee table.

Sofia took Kim's and Debbie's jackets and motioned for them to sit. After she served the cake and tea, she left her teacup and cake on the coffee table and leaned back against the sofa. She took a paper from her apron pocket. "I received my DNA test results this morning." She glanced at the paper. "It says '42 percent South France, 29 percent North France, 12 percent Northeast France, 8 percent Northwest France, 6 percent Italy, and 3 percent Germany.'" She looked up. "I have matches for biological relatives in France, but I have none in the US that aren't distant. I can only conclude that Robert Jennings is not my biological father."

"Yes," Kim said. "It sounds as if that is the reasonable conclusion."

Debbie nodded in agreement.

"I was trying to digest that today as I baked the cake. This afternoon, I returned to the storage room in the basement, where I've been going through a bookcase that Daddy built years ago. The bottom shelves have doors on them. I thought it was full of old textbooks of mine from college and teaching, but I found something in the far back corner." She pointed to what looked like a book on the table under the window. "It's very heavy."

"I couldn't get it out of the bookcase. I finally had to ask my neighbor to help me, and then he carried it upstairs. It's not a book at all. It's some sort of box with a keyhole for a very small key." Sofia took another piece of paper from her apron pocket. "I decided to keep cleaning out the bookcase to see if I could find anything else related to the box." She opened the piece of paper. "I didn't find a key, but I did find this tucked between two French books." She held up the paper. "It's a letter from Mama, written in April of 2005. I'm guessing she forgot all about it the last few years."

Debbie leaned forward in her chair in anticipation.

Sofia began to read. "*Ma chérie*, Sofia, I have wanted to tell you this at least a hundred times over the last sixty years, but then each time changed my mind. Finally, after much prayer, I decided to leave a letter. If you find it, it is meant to be for you to know. If not, I'll take these secrets to my grave.

"'Robert Jennings was your father, from the moment he first took you in his arms. You adored him almost as much as he adored you. But your biological father was Raphael Chappelle, a fellow art student who fought in 1940 against the Germans. He was captured and held in a German camp for several months and then escaped and made his way back to Paris, to me.

"'My father had a shipping company in Marseilles and, as you've probably surmised, was quite wealthy. Once the war started, my parents begged me to return home, but I refused. I needed to wait for Raphael in Paris. I worked as a nanny for a wealthy family until the Germans invaded. Then I worked as a maid in the same house for the Nazi officers who had seized it.

"'Raphael worked as a waiter, and we were both part of the French Resistance, gathering information from our jobs and sending messages in drawings. I tried to leave you a message in a painting, but it was taken at the only exhibit I had in Dennison. The painting wasn't even on exhibit. It was in a box with other items.

"'Once Germany invaded France, my parents tried once again to get me to return to Marseilles. My father had educated me to work in his business. I was good with numbers, and I'd studied English since I was a girl, but I knew by then he was collaborating with the Nazis. I couldn't go back, no matter how hungry I grew in Paris.

"'Raphael and I married in 1944, although we weren't able to live together until after we were liberated in August of 1944. I was pregnant with you by then. We thought we'd made it and our happily-ever-after was around the corner, once the war ended and life returned to normal. We would have our baby and resume our studies. But then Raphael fell ill in November with an infection from a wound he sustained on a resistance trip he took to Normandy right after D-Day. The wound became septic, and he died within a few days.

"'I met Bob Jennings in December of 1944 at the hotel where I'd gotten a job as a maid. He was in Paris for R & R. Bob was kind and caring, unlike some of the other soldiers who stayed at the hotel.

"'We told you your birthday was July 7, 1945, but you were actually born on January 13, 1945. Soon after that, Bob was transferred to Paris for a short assignment in an office and found me through the hotel. Another young woman and I shared an apartment and looked after each other's babies so we could at least work part-time as maids. You and I were both undernourished and had respiratory infections. Bob found medical care for us. He said he had younger siblings and couldn't turn his back on a baby although he was only twenty at the time, a year younger than I was—but we'd both been through so much. We were older than our years. Because I could speak English and type, Bob got me a job in the American office where he worked. I made enough to hire a neighbor woman to care for you. He was being sent back to the front in March. Before he left, he asked me to marry him, and I said yes. Did I love him? I'm not sure. I certainly respected him. And appreciated him. Perhaps I was too exhausted, too hungry, too afraid, to refuse him. But I came to love him very much.

"'We never planned to deceive you about your parentage. We planned to tell you when you were five or six. But my reception in Dennison was dubious. And the rumors soon started, claiming Bob wasn't your father. Claiming I'd tricked him. If they would treat me, a grown woman, that way, how would you be treated? We kept putting off telling you until, finally, we simply didn't. I never forgot Raphael, never stopped mourning him, but I stopped being aware you ever had a father besides Bob.

"'I never met Raphael's family. They lived in a small village in Normandy. His mother and father were killed during the war. His sister disappeared. But perhaps somewhere in France, you have cousins. Relatives.

"'The clues in the painting that disappeared were meant to lead you to a box of gold coins from Raphael. His grandfather, who lived in Paris before the war, gave them to him. He left them for you. I never told Bob about them, for no other reason than that it felt good to have a story about Raphael that was mine. He thought my trunk from France was heavy because of the books I'd brought—and I did bring books, my art books from school. But I also brought the coins. Ask Eileen for her help. I gave her a message for you years ago.

"'Please forgive me for keeping these stories. My intentions were good, although I understand the outcome may not be.

"'But also know how much both Rafael and Bob loved you and how much you blessed us. You were my hope. You were what kept me going after your father died. And you were the one who gave me the courage to say yes to your daddy and move halfway around the world.

"'*Je t'aime de tout mon coeur.*'" Sofia paused a moment and then added, "She signed it, 'Mama.'" Sofia folded the letter. "And unless someone moved it, I'm guessing the key is in the model depot."

CHAPTER TWENTY-ONE

ebbie woke the next morning at six to a text from Mom. HAPPY BIRTHDAY TO YOU, HAPPY BIRTHDAY TO YOU, HAPPY BIRTHDAY DEAR DEBBIE, HAPPY BIRTHDAY TO YOU!

After rolling out of bed, Debbie responded to the text and then got ready for her day, more determined than ever to find the model depot and the painting. They had to locate the key for Sofia and help her discover the gold coins and any more information about her past that might exist.

When Debbie arrived at the café, Janet had a candle-topped fruit tart on the counter along with a latte. "Happy birthday!" she called out. "Welcome to halfway to eighty-eight!"

Debbie groaned. "You know how to ruin a girl's day, don't you?"

Janet poured herself a cup of coffee. "I do my best. Now, don't hang around in the kitchen today. I've already baked the cake, but I'm going to get it decorated before I leave for the day. Ask Paulette to pick up the orders." She grinned. "You handle things on the floor."

"Got it." Debbie took a sip of her latte. "I thought I'd sneak out after ten and see if Esther is working at the library. I have a few questions for her."

"All right," Janet said. "Any updates?"

"Actually…" Debbie told her about the box Sofia had found and the letter. "Sofia always thought she was born in July of 1945, but it turns out she was born in January. Her parents adjusted her birthday so no one would question if Bob was her father until they were ready to tell her. She was so little no one questioned her age."

"Is Sofia going to break into the box if the key isn't found?" Janet asked.

"She tried to pick the lock yesterday but wasn't successful. She's going to call a locksmith this morning, but she really hopes the depot is found."

Debbie leaned against the counter. "Oh, and listen to this." She told Janet about getting to the bottom of things with Jaxon and Julian—that they both suspected and protected the other—and then about Kristy telling Greg the model depot had been found, only to find out that wasn't the case and that some sort of miscommunication—whether accidental or intentional—had taken place. "At this point, the two suspects who are left are Kristy and Carson. One or the other, or perhaps both."

Janet picked up her cup of coffee and took a step toward the kitchen. "Well, maybe Esther can shed some light on the connection between the two Jennings families."

"I hope so."

The morning progressed quickly, and at ten, Debbie said goodbye to Janet and Paulette and headed to the Uhrichsville branch of the Claymont Public Library.

When she arrived, she didn't see anyone matching Janet's description of Esther, so she asked the librarian if the woman was volunteering.

"She is," the librarian said. "She's in the archives. She'll be out soon."

Debbie browsed a display on local books—one about Camp Dennison and another on the pioneer days of Ohio. After about five minutes, she looked up and saw a woman with gray hair pulled back in a ponytail carrying a stack of books to the desk. The librarian said something and gestured to Debbie.

Debbie smiled as the woman came toward her. "I'm Debbie Albright. Are you Esther Wilcox?"

"Yes," the woman said. "It's nice to meet you. How can I help you?"

"Do you mind if I ask you a few questions about the Jennings family?"

"Not at all," Esther said. "We can speak at the table in the corner."

Debbie followed her and sat down in the chair closest to the one Esther chose, hoping their conversation wouldn't be overheard by anyone nearby.

"Are you a friend of the woman who was in here last week doing research on Marguerite Jennings?"

"Yes," Debbie said. "Janet told me what you said about Sofia Jennings."

Esther sighed. "I shouldn't have said that."

"Why did you?"

"I don't know. It's a rumor from so long ago. One reason may be that I feel I missed out on ever knowing Sofia. We were second cousins, so maybe we wouldn't have known each other well anyway. But my mother stopped any chance I might have ever had."

"What's the other reason?"

"I believe it was more than a rumor that she wasn't Bob Jennings's biological daughter. Doesn't everyone have a right to know their own history?"

Debbie didn't confirm that Esther was correct. It wasn't her business to do that. Instead, she asked, "How did your mother stop you from getting to know Sofia?"

Esther shifted her gaze to the window. "My mother had her problems. It took me a long time to realize how bad they were. She was beautiful—auburn hair, striking dark eyes, dark eyebrows. She wore bright red lipstick as if it were 1943 her entire life. She was beautiful but very self-centered. If she was in love with Bob Jennings, it was a love he didn't return. She couldn't seem to forgive him when he married a French woman and then brought her to Dennison. I think it hurt her pride. A few years later she married my father, Stephen Jennings, but the marriage didn't last long. Then she married again. She wasn't happy with her second marriage either, but she stuck it out.

"One time, when I was about five, she took me to *Lady and the Tramp*. We saw a family—a father, mother, and a girl who was older than me—as we left the theater. My mother said something to them, although I couldn't figure out what it was. But her words hurt the mother and confused the girl. And it made the man angry. He told her to leave his wife and daughter alone. When we got home, I asked her who they were. She said the woman was a Frenchie who'd stolen a treasure and had tricked the man into marrying her and that the girl wasn't his. As a child, I had no idea what she was talking about, but through the years, as I heard rumors about the family, it made more sense. Then, as an adult, I wondered if my mother had started the rumors.

"Years later, my mother told my nephew that Marguerite Jennings had stolen the treasure from *her*. Somehow, her story morphed from Marguerite stealing a treasure to Marguerite stealing the treasure from her, from my mother." Esther shook her head as if she was still in disbelief. "By the time my nephew was in grade school, my mother lived with me. He'd stay with me after school, and she was always telling him stories about all sorts of things, many of them true. About how she moved to Dennison when she was in high school and then, after she graduated, worked at the Depot canteen.

"She told him how she wrote to soldiers and sailors who were stationed all over the world. And then she told him the wild stories about Marguerite. Somehow, who knows how exactly, she came across a painting of the depot that had all sorts of strange things in it. Keys and mirrors and coins. Nicely done but bizarre. She told my nephew that the painting had to do with her stolen gold, and then she gave the painting to him. He adored her—she spoiled him, and he believed every word she said. She died when he was ten, and he mourned her more than any of us."

Debbie eyes grew wider with each segment of Esther's story, but she didn't respond.

"I suppose it all paid off in that my nephew now writes about the railroad system across the US during World War II and he's researching Dennison and the depot," Esther said.

Debbie's heart began to race. Carson. Carson was related to Sofia.

"But I shouldn't have let my mother have such a big influence on him." Esther gave Debbie a wry smile. "Anyway, when Janet came looking into the Jennings family, I couldn't help but speak up."

"Thank you," Debbie said. "First, I should say I know your nephew. Carson Argyle. He and I went to school together and have reconnected since he and Kristy moved back to Dennison."

"Oh, that's nice. I'm thankful to have them here, especially since his mother, my sister, Priscilla, and her husband moved to Cleveland. Carson is a good person. I just regret letting my mother influence him, although she was a good cook and passed that down to Carson."

Wasn't that the way life went? The good with the bad? The cooking skills along with lies about Marguerite Jennings and a missing treasure. "Do you know what happened to the painting?" Debbie asked.

Esther grimaced. "Don't tell Carson." She lowered her voice. "He left it at my house, and it ended up in a giveaway box. I thought he was done with it, but a few years ago he asked about it. I told him I had no idea what became of it. I most likely donated it somewhere."

And most likely Carson has it again, Debbie thought.

"I slipped into the back of Marguerite's funeral, just to pay my respects. Sofia didn't have any family with her, and that made me sad."

"It's not too late to reach out to Sofia," Debbie said. "I don't know how she would respond, but she might welcome the gesture."

"Do you think so?"

Debbie nodded. "It's worth a try," she said. "Sofia is a lovely woman. She loved Bob Jennings very much. He was a wonderful father. He and Marguerite raised Sofia to be a good person, full of empathy. She took care of both of her parents and now is trying to tie up loose ends from their—and her—past."

"Well, thank you," Esther said. "I'm glad I told Janet what I did, and I'm thankful she told you. It's been good to talk it through. You've been a good listener."

"Thank you for telling me," Debbie said. "It's helped me too." Although she didn't know exactly how helpful the information would be—at least not yet.

Eight hours later, Debbie sat at Kristy and Carson's dining room table with Mom, Dad, Ian, Janet, Greg, Kim, and Barry, Kim's husband. And Kristy and Carson.

Debbie had never felt so duplicitous.

A bouquet of orange roses sat in the middle of the table, which was covered by a chocolate-brown tablecloth. They ate off ivory china and drank from crystal glasses. Kristy had affixed silk leaves in reds, oranges, and yellows, intertwined with twinkle lights, to the molding around the dining room ceiling.

The entire setting was enchanting. As Debbie took her last bite of the Mediterranean chicken Carson had made, Kristy said, "I can't wait for Janet to reveal her cake." She smiled at Debbie. "You're going to love it."

Debbie returned the smile, but inside she churned. She should have canceled the dinner. What would Kristy and Carson think of her once she proved one of them—or both—took the model depot? *If* she could prove that one of them—or both—took it. She didn't want to make an accusation and then be wrong again, as she had been so many years ago.

A few minutes later, Kristy and Carson began gathering the dinner plates. Mom hopped up to clear the food, followed by Dad.

"I'll go get the cake ready to serve," Janet said. "Come on, Ian. I need some help."

Kim got up to help clear the table too. Debbie gave her a look and then stood.

"No, no," Kristy said. "You're the birthday girl. Besides, no one wants you to see the cake."

That was true. Paulette wouldn't let Debbie in the kitchen all afternoon—not until Janet left with the cake in a box.

Debbie and Greg made small talk while the others worked. In just a few minutes the table was set for coffee and dessert, and Janet ceremoniously brought in an orange-and-white striped cake with orange confetti along the bottom and orange macarons arranged on the top with laser-cut gold letters spelling out Happy Birthday sticking up above the cake.

Debbie began clapping, and the others joined in. "It's beautiful. Thank you," Debbie said, standing and giving Janet a hug. Then she hugged Carson and Kristy. "Thank you for this wonderful dinner. It's all been so lovely. I can't thank you enough."

Janet handed Debbie the knife. "I'm not making you blow out forty-four candles, but you do get to cut the cake."

"Gladly," Debbie said.

A few minutes later, after Kristy led them in singing "Happy Birthday," they were all seated at the table again, eating the chocolate cake with orange and vanilla frosting.

"Tell me about the little hideaway in the backyard," Mom said to Kristy. "Is it your office?"

"No," she said. "It's Carson's."

"A man cave?"

"More like an office," Carson said. "I can spread out my books and files and not have to worry about cleaning up all the time. Otherwise, I'd have everything spread out over this table."

"It's true," Kristy said. "My work is tidy and hardly takes up any room. Carson needs the extra space."

"So what was the deal with someone saying the depot was found when it wasn't?" Kim asked out of the blue.

"What?" Kristy appeared shocked. "It hasn't been found?" She turned to Carson. "You told me it was."

Alarmed, Debbie pulled her phone from her pocket. Kristy had texted her last night that the depot hadn't turned up.

"I misunderstood," Carson said. "And forgot to tell you."

Debbie gawked at Carson and then Kristy. What was going on?

"What about the painting?" Kristy asked. "Was it not found either?"

Carson lowered his voice. "I never told you the painting was found."

"Yes, you did."

Debbie held her phone up. "Kristy, I texted you last night. You texted back." She swiped her screen and found the text. Oops, FALSE ALARM. THE DEPOT HASN'T BEEN FOUND. SORRY. THE OTHER VOLUNTEER MISUNDERSTOOD KIM. She passed her phone to Kristy.

She read it and then said, "I didn't write that text." She turned to Carson. "You answered that when you were looking at pictures on my phone, right? And then deleted the texts. Why would you do that?"

"Let's talk about this later." He kept his voice low. "There's no need to ruin the party."

"Actually, I think it would be good if we talked about it now," Debbie said.

"No." Kristy stood. "Carson's right. We don't need to talk anymore." She headed to the kitchen.

Debbie followed. Kristy grabbed a key by the back door and then, with BG barking at her heels, hurried outside.

Carson stepped into the kitchen. "Kristy!"

Debbie looked from Carson to the backyard and took off after Kristy.

CHAPTER TWENTY-TWO

Kristy had the door unlocked and open by the time Debbie reached the office. She stepped inside and flipped on a light. Debbie hurried after her.

"There it is." Kristy stepped to the middle of the room and pointed. On the top of a bookcase was the model of an old train and the model depot. Below it on the bookcase was Ray's painting.

"I can explain," Carson said as he stepped into the office, followed by Ian.

Kristy turned to him. "You lied to me."

Carson stood like a dejected child, arms limp at his sides and eyes downcast. "I got in over my head."

Janet was next to come into the office and then Kim. Greg stopped outside the door.

Carson continued speaking. "And yes, I was deceptive, but I never meant to lie to you."

"What about the painting? You stole that."

"It's mine. My grandmother gave it to me."

"How about if Kim, Debbie, Carson, and I have a chat?" Ian said. "Everyone else, go back in and have another cup of decaf. We'll get this figured out."

Janet stepped into the office, put her arm around Kristy, and led her out. Greg followed them to the back door of the house, where Mom and Dad stood.

Ian closed the door to the office.

Debbie took a second to look around. It definitely had a railroad theme. On the walls were vintage photographs of trains from all over the US—going through a mountain pass, along a lake, through a city. There was a recliner in one corner and a rocking chair in another. Carson's desk was covered with papers and books, and a folding table, covered with more books and papers, sat next to the desk.

Carson sat down in the desk chair while Ian leaned against the table. Kim sat in the recliner, and Debbie sat in the rocking chair.

"Tell us what happened," Ian said.

Carson shrugged. "I did take the depot. I intended to return it the next morning before anyone realized it was gone. I didn't know that Kim planned to take it to someone that night. I also took the painting, but it was already mine."

"Can anyone corroborate that?" Ian asked.

"I can," Debbie said. "At least, it once belonged to him."

Both Ian and Carson gave her questioning looks.

"I spoke with Carson's aunt, Esther Wilcox, this morning, and she told me about the painting. She put it in a giveaway box."

Carson hit his forehead with the heel of his hand.

Debbie nodded toward Kim. "We spoke with Sofia Jennings, who happens to be Esther's second cousin—and Carson's more distant cousin—and we're certain that this painting was created by Marguerite Jennings and taken from her when she was exhibiting her work."

Carson shook his head.

Debbie continued speaking. "After talking with Esther, I think it's likely that her mother took the painting."

"No," said Carson.

"I'm afraid so," said Debbie. "Then, after your aunt gave it away, at some point Ray Zink bought it."

Carson ran his hand down the side of his face. "I really messed up, didn't I?"

"It sounds, according to your aunt," Debbie said, "as if your grandmother fed you a bunch of lies about a treasure chest of gold coins."

"And a key in the depot," Carson said. "Except it's not there. I checked."

Kim stood and pointed to the depot. "Mind if I look?" she asked Ian.

"Of course not," he said. "This isn't a criminal investigation, unless you want to press charges."

"I don't. Although I can't speak for Ray." Kim stepped to the bookcase and picked up the depot. She peered inside and shook it, but it didn't make a sound. She handed it to Debbie.

She shook it too. "Did you take the roof off?" she asked Carson.

"I did. There's no key."

Debbie frowned. "Does Sofia still need the key?"

"Yes," Kim said. "The locksmith is out of town until Monday."

"We should take this to her," Debbie said. "She might have an idea about how her mother hid it."

"Let's go right now," Kim said. "Then we can return to the party and tell everyone goodbye." She glanced at Ian. "What about Carson?"

"We'll stay out here," Ian said. "Kristy might need a little more time before he goes back in the house."

Debbie unlocked the doors to her car as Kim called Sofia to tell her they were on their way to her house with the model depot.

Sofia stood at the door waiting for them. "You found it," she said as Debbie and Kim hurried up the steps.

Kim held it up so Sofia could see.

"It looks like it's in good shape," Sofia said.

"It is." Together, as they walked into the house, Debbie and Kim told her what happened. "We're hoping, if the key is still inside the depot, you can find it."

Sofia took the depot and walked into the dining room. She turned on the overhead light and a reading lamp on the table. "I'll get some tools." She walked out of the dining room and through the kitchen. A few minutes later she returned, sat down, and began running her hands along the seams of the depot.

"Carson said he took off the roof but didn't find anything," Debbie said.

Sofia picked up a detail knife and popped the roof off. "That would be my first guess too."

Debbie wasn't sure why Sofia was looking under the roof if Carson hadn't found anything. Sofia held the roof up. There was nothing on the underside. Then she picked up the knife again and pried against the roof. A panel popped out. "It's a very thin false ceiling." Sofia held up the roof again. Glued to the underside of it was a small key.

Sofia used the knife to pry the key from the wood, and then the three women quickly hurried to the table in the living room. Sofia put the key into the lock of the box that looked like a book. She turned it. Nothing happened. Then she wiggled it, and there was a small click. She attempted to open the lid, and at first it didn't budge. Then she shimmied it and tried again. The lid lifted.

Debbie took a step closer. On top there was a large envelope with a button and string closure, something she hadn't seen since she was a child in her grandparents' house.

Sofia lifted it, revealing brown packing paper below it. She opened the envelope, pulled out two documents, and studied the first one. "This is my French birth certificate. Like Mama said in her letter, I was born January 13, 1945. I'm guessing they didn't submit this when they applied for my US birth certificate." She read the second document. "This is their French marriage certificate. They got married on March 10, 1945, two months after I was born." She slid her hand back in the envelope and brought out a black-and-white photo of a young soldier, a headshot that appeared to be a professional photo. He wore a French uniform and a beret over his dark hair. He grinned for the camera, his eyes lively. He appeared to be the young man in the drawings Sofia had found earlier. She flipped the photo over and read, "Raphael Sofus Chappelle, 1939." Her voice choked as she said, "Sofus. I was named after him."

Kim gave Sofia a hug. Debbie patted her back, relieved that Sofia had found more of her story.

"Well," Sofia said, "any guesses on whether there are gold coins beneath the packing paper?"

"I can't wait to find out," Debbie said. Everything else that Marguerite's painting and letter declared was true. She guessed the existence of the coins was too.

Sofia lifted the packing paper, revealing several rows of gold coins. She put her hands to her chest.

"Don't touch them," Kim said. "I have a pair of archival gloves in my purse." Once Sofia had put them on, she picked up a coin. It had the image of a man on it.

"Is that Napoleon?" Debbie asked.

Sofia nodded. She turned the coin over and read, "40 franc. 1807." She looked up. "How do we find out how much they're worth?"

"A coin shop in Columbus could tell you." Debbie took her phone from her purse. "I'll see what I can find online for a general idea." A couple of sites popped up. "This one says $799." She clicked on the next. "$850. Here's another. $875. If we go with the middle estimate, these are worth about $85,000."

"Congratulations," Kim said. "That's certainly enough for a new roof and other repairs."

Tears filled Sofia's eyes as she held the coin against her chest. "*Dieu merci*," she whispered. "Thank You, God."

Saturday morning, Janet and Paulette had been at the café making doughnuts for a couple of hours by the time Debbie joined them. Once Madison arrived, Debbie went to Good Shepherd and returned the painting to Ray. Kim had called Eileen the evening before and told her the depot—and the key—had been found.

"Eileen told me all about what happened," Ray said as he held the painting in his hands. "She's on her way to Sofia's right now." He gestured to the artwork. "Of course, we won't tell anyone about the gold coins. We don't want anyone else trying to take what rightfully belongs to Sofia."

"Definitely," Debbie said.

"In fact," Ray said, "I'll give this painting back to her as well. Eileen is going to invite her to Sunday lunch tomorrow. I'll give it to her then."

"Good idea," Debbie said. "Mind if I join you? I'd love to see her face when she sees the original painting."

"Of course," Ray said. "You're always welcome."

Soon after Debbie returned to the café, Kristy walked in and sat at the counter. "Good morning," Debbie said. "How are you?"

"All right." Kristy smiled. "Your pumpkin spice latte will help. Make it to go, please."

"You got it," Debbie answered.

Once it was made and in Kristy's hands, she said, "Carson and I have been hashing things out. He's mortified—and I'm not as angry as I was last night. He thinks we should probably move back to Chicago."

"Do you want to move back?"

Kristy shook her head. "But I wish he'd told me the crazy stuff his grandmother told him growing up. I thought he had a good childhood."

"He did have a good childhood," Debbie said. "But it's too bad his parents didn't know what Anna was telling him. Or that Esther didn't realize the impact Anna had."

"He's an adult now," Kristy said. "He's responsible for what he does. He really messed up."

"If you want to stay here, I hope you will," Debbie said. "You'll find a lot of grace and understanding in this community. You'll find people who'll walk beside you and love you." Debbie smiled. "Starting with me. I'd really like another chance at being your friend."

"Ditto." Kristy's eyes glistened. Debbie stepped around the counter and gave Kristy a hug, wiping her own tears away as she did.

Ten minutes later, Julian burst into the café, followed by Greg and Jaxon. "We have tickets for the train," Julian called out to Debbie. "Want to come with us?"

"Aw, I'm working," Debbie said.

"No you're not."

Debbie turned and saw Janet standing behind the counter.

"It's part of your birthday present," Janet said. "We've got this covered."

Paulette grinned and gave Julian a big ol' grandma hug. Then she hugged Greg and gave Jaxon as much of a hug as he would let her.

Madison started toward the kitchen with a stack of plates. "Hi, Jaxon," she said as she passed him.

"Hi," he replied.

Julian stepped closer to Debbie. "Can Madison go with us?"

"I'm working," Madison said.

"Yes, but you're going to work on the train," Janet informed her. "Kim said the volunteer needs help passing out the cookies."

"Really?" Madison broke into a smile. Jaxon smiled back at her.

"You all have fun! Come in for lunch when you're done," Paulette said.

Greg gave his mother another hug while Debbie and Madison headed to the kitchen to hang up their aprons and wash their hands.

A half hour later the whistle blew, and the train began to roll. This time it picked up speed quicker, and they were soon out of town, into the trees where the leaves were even more spectacular than the Saturday before.

In the row behind Debbie, the three young people chattered away.

"Thank you," Greg said to Debbie, his voice low, "for helping me figure out the stuff with the boys on Thursday. After we got home that night, they both said they appreciated how calm you were about everything."

"Really?"

He nodded. "Thanks for not giving up on them."

Debbie's heart warmed as the train gained more speed. Her thoughts turned to Bob Jennings. Sofia had been a baby when he and Marguerite married. Sofia had never known another father. But Bob had risen to the task and embraced being a parent. Then she thought of Amanda Dunn and of Brent and Monty asking her to refer to herself as their mother. Maybe being a stepparent wasn't as hard as Debbie feared. Not that she had any idea of what the future held for her. Or Greg. Or his boys. But it wouldn't hurt to be open to what God had planned, no matter what that was.

Greg nudged her with his shoulder. "Thank you too for not giving up on me when things get crazy, like they did this week."

Debbie nudged him back as "I'll Be Seeing You" began playing over the sound system. She and Greg had a sweet friendship, and she was content with that. At least for the moment.

She'd trust God for what came next.

Dear Reader,

Two components in the Whistle Stop Café series deeply resonate with me: 1) the backstory focused on World War II, and 2) that Debbie, one of the main characters, lost her fiancé in Afghanistan. Why? My father was a World War II veteran, and my husband is a veteran of the war in Afghanistan. One shaped my past as a child, and the other shaped my present as an adult.

Thankfully, they both survived and also documented their experiences. My father, Bruce Egger, kept a diary during his service time, which he completed after the war ended. He also saved all his letters, as did his parents and his little sister. His memories became part of the book *G Company's War*, which he coauthored with Lee Otts.

My husband also kept a diary during his time in Afghanistan, and I saved all our emails, plus all the articles and video clips about his unit. At the time of this writing, we've done nothing with those documents besides preserve them. As we discover with the characters in the Whistle Stop Café series, it takes years to process the experiences of war. (My father didn't write his World War II memories until he was in his sixties, after he retired.) But what my husband and I have processed and hold dear was God's constancy in keeping us close to each other and close to Him through that time.

As I wrote *I'll Be Seeing You*, my father and his war buddies, along with my husband and his, were on my mind, along with all of us on the home front during both conflicts. I hope as you read, you'll be thinking of your loved ones who were affected and shaped by war, no matter how they served.

Enjoy!

Leslie Gould

ABOUT the AUTHOR

*L*eslie Gould is the number-one bestselling and Christy-Award winning author of over forty novels. She's also won two Faith, Hope, and Love Readers' Choice Awards and has been a finalist for the Carol Award. Leslie has a bachelor's degree in history and a Master of Fine Arts degree in creative writing. In the past, she curated the Swedenburg House Museum in Ashland, Oregon, edited a magazine, and taught writing on the university level. Currently, she writes and edits full-time. She and her husband, Peter, live in Portland, Oregon, and enjoy hiking, traveling, and spending time with their adult children and grandbaby.

TRUTH BEHIND the FICTION

*L*ove and war go together. Not surprisingly, World War II was no exception, resulting in American servicemen falling in love with and marrying women from Europe to Asia during and after the war. As Eileen explains in *I'll Be Seeing You*, between the War Brides Act of 1945 and the Alien Fiancées and Fiancés Act of 1946 and 1947, nearly 300,000 women (who either married or were engaged to US military men) and their dependents arrived in the US before the expiration of the acts in 1948. One of the books I read while researching this story was *French War Brides in America: an Oral History* by Hilary Kaiser, who stated that the overall number included approximately 6,000 French war brides.

The women settled all over the country—in cities, towns, and rural areas. Besides adjusting to marriages with men some of them barely knew, the brides adjusted to a second or additional language and a new culture while mourning the tragedies of war and all they had left behind. However, nearly all, in one way or another, lived the American dream and assimilated into their new country. They became businesswomen, professors, artists, and so much more.

I imagined Marguerite, who arrives by train in Dennison with her daughter in *I'll Be Seeing You*, into existence as a representation of the French war brides from World War II. Although Marguerite meets some resistance in her new community, she also receives love and acceptance from Eileen and others, allowing her to carve out a meaningful life in Dennison. In the end, Marguerite gives as much to her new community as she receives, as did the real-life French war brides who came to the US nearly eighty years ago.

FROM the HOME-FRONT KITCHEN

Caramel Apple Tarts
(makes 12)

Ingredients for the dough:

2 cups all-purpose flour

¾ cup unsalted butter cut
    into cubes

3 tablespoons brown sugar

¾ teaspoon salt

3 tablespoons water

Ingredients for the apple filling:

2 tablespoons unsalted butter

5–6 large apples, peeled, cored,
    and sliced

½ cup granulated sugar

¼ cup brown sugar

1 teaspoon ground cinnamon

½ teaspoon ground allspice

¼ teaspoon ground ginger

¼ teaspoon salt

2 tablespoons all-purpose flour

2 tablespoons cornstarch

1 tablespoon lemon juice

Ingredients for the caramel:

1 14-oz package individually
    wrapped caramels,
    unwrapped

1 (5 ounce) can evaporated
    milk

Instructions:

For dough:

1. Add flour, butter, brown sugar, and salt to food processor. Pulse several times until crumbly mixture forms.
2. Add 2–3 tablespoons water and pulse until dough comes together in a ball.
3. Divide dough into 6 equal pieces. Flatten each piece into a disc and wrap with plastic wrap. Refrigerate dough for at least 1 hour. (Note: dough can be made the day before and refrigerated overnight.)

For filling:

1. Melt butter in large, deep skillet over medium-high heat.
2. Once butter has melted, add apples, sugar, brown sugar, cinnamon, allspice, ginger, and salt; stir until well combined. Cook for 5 to 7 minutes or until apples have begun to soften.
3. Add flour and cornstarch; stir until well combined. Continue cooking, stirring occasionally, 4 to 5 minutes.
4. Transfer apples into a medium bowl. Add lemon juice; stir until well combined. Let mixture cool completely.

For caramel:

1. Combine caramels and evaporated milk in medium saucepan over low heat and cook, stirring often, until mixture is smooth.

For tarts:

1. Preheat oven to 375 degrees.
2. Working on a lightly floured surface, roll each piece of dough into 4" circle.
3. Place ¼ cup of apple filling into center of each circle and fold edges of dough towards the center.

4. Place each tart into a muffin tin.

5. Pour caramel into center of each tart.

6. Bake for 28 to 30 minutes, or until edges of tarts are golden brown.

7. Let cool for 30 minutes before serving.

Read on for a sneak peek of another exciting book
in the Whistle Stop Café Mysteries series!

FOOLS RUSH IN

BY BETH ADAMS

The sky was dark velvet, pricked with spots of golden light. Dawn was still more than an hour away, and the air was crisp and cold. *Fall is here, there's no doubt about that,* Janet Shaw thought as she walked down the steps and into the kitchen. Her husband, Ian, was still asleep and would be for hours. She filled Ranger's bowl with cat food and refilled Laddie's water dish, pulled on her coat, and stepped outside. The neighborhood was quiet, the streets still. Janet loved this time of day, when the world was silent and it felt like it belonged just to her.

She started the car, and the engine hummed. She flipped on her lights and looked around, and then she backed out of the driveway as the air inside the car started to warm. It wasn't a long drive to the Whistle Stop Café, but walking it at this hour would be asking a bit too much.

The car was making a weird banging noise. Ian had promised to take a look at it but hadn't had the chance. For now, she ignored it, and as she drove through the sleepy streets of the small town of Dennison, she made a mental list of the game plan for the day. She'd get the piecrusts made and chilling first, and then she'd turn her attention to the day's other baked goods. She was thinking cranberry and white chocolate for the scones, plus the traditional plain and blueberry. And some pumpkin spice muffins were in order—those would sell well on a crisp fall day like today. Oh, and she could make apple cinnamon too, topped with a sugar and cinnamon crumble. She would make a batch of doughnuts as well… She was getting hungry just thinking about them. But first, coffee. She'd get it started as soon as she got in. Coffee made the early mornings bearable.

Janet would never stop being grateful she'd been able to open the Whistle Stop Café with her best friend, Debbie Albright, in the old train depot. Janet had worked in a bakery in Uhrichsville for years, but owning a business with Debbie was a dream come true. They'd been doing great since they opened this past summer and had already developed a steady stream of loyal customers.

Janet parked the car and walked up to the old train depot. It appeared a murky brown in the dim predawn light but was actually a vintage redbrick and stone structure. The café was at the west end of the building, and she started toward it—

But wait. Why was a light on inside? It looked bright and cheerful, casting the interior of the café in a warm glow, but Janet knew this was a big problem. There shouldn't be any lights on in the café at this hour. She walked faster. Had they left them on when they'd closed down yesterday? She didn't think so. Someone would have noticed before now, wouldn't they? But was it possible—

She stopped short. The door was open. She and Debbie definitely hadn't left the door open. And there was something shiny on the ground at the base of the door. Was that—

She stifled a shriek when she saw that the glinting was the light from inside being reflected on broken glass. The glass that used to be part of the door.

Should she go in? But what if whoever had done this was still there? No way. She wasn't going in there. Not alone, anyway. Janet pulled out her phone and dialed quickly.

"Hello?" Ian's voice was groggy.

"Ian?" Janet's husband was the local chief of police.

"Janet? What's going on?" Now Ian was on full alert.

"I think someone broke into the café. The door is open, the light is on, and there's glass on the ground. I'm afraid to go in there."

"Stay outside," he said. She could hear him moving around. "Don't go in, and don't hang up. I'm staying on the line, and I'll be right there."

Janet held her phone to her ear, staring at the café, trying to make sense of what she was seeing. So many people in town seemed delighted to have the old depot open and serving food again, just like it had all those decades ago. Who would do something like this? She bit her lip, trying to stay calm.

A few minutes later headlights swept around the corner, and Ian parked his car and jumped out. He must have sped the whole way, but she was glad he'd come so quickly. She realized she was shaking.

"Are you okay?" Ian asked, walking toward her.

"I'm fine," Janet said. "I didn't go inside."

"I'll check it out. You stay here until I tell you it's clear." Ian walked to the café and pushed the door farther open with his toe. It scraped across the broken glass on the ground, but it opened. He edged his way in, on high alert, and peered around the café's dining area, behind the counter, and into the kitchen. After a moment Janet saw him come out of the café and go through the doors that led to the museum section of the depot. Then, finally, he came back out.

"It's clear. You can come in, but don't touch anything."

Janet stepped through the open door and bit back a cry. It was even worse than it had looked from outside. Several tables were overturned, tossed carelessly on top of one another. More than one chair leg was broken. But that wasn't the worst part. The worst was that the walls—the ones they had so lovingly painted a sunny yellow and hung with vintage photos of the depot in its heyday—had been covered with ugly red spray paint. Someone had painted zigzags and other random designs all over the walls and even over the pictures. And—oh my. One of the pictures was missing, and a spray-painted crown had been left in its place.

"They tried to break into this," Ian said. He stood over the cash register, shining a flashlight at the edge. Janet went over and saw that he was pointing at a place where the paint had been scraped away. "It doesn't look like they succeeded."

"I'm glad of that," Janet said. "Though there's nothing in it. We empty it and put the cash in the safe every day when we close." Thank goodness. At least they hadn't lost hundreds of dollars on top of whatever it was going to cost to get this place fixed up. Insurance would cover at least some of it, she hoped.

"Where's the safe?" Ian asked.

"It's in the back."

"Why don't you go check to make sure it's still locked. Just don't touch it."

"I won't." Janet hurried to the kitchen to where the safe was tucked under a counter. She was relieved to see that it was closed. Only she and Debbie knew the combination. She walked back into the café. "They didn't get into it," she said."

Ian nodded. He used his phone to take a picture of the marks on the cash register. "I'm glad to hear that."

Janet heard sirens, and a moment later a Dennison Police Department cruiser came blazing into the parking lot, its blue and red lights strobing in the pre-dawn gloom. When had Ian called the station? Deputy Brendan Vaughn stepped out of the vehicle and rushed into the café. He was tall and had close-cropped brown hair.

"Good work getting here so quickly," Ian said to him. "Looks like someone was hoping for a quick payday." He gestured toward the cash register. "They didn't get anything though."

"That's good news," Deputy Vaughn said. "Should I start dusting for prints?"

Brendan Vaughn was only a few years out of the police academy and looked like he spent a lot of time at the gym. Janet knew several single women in town who had their eye on him.

"It probably won't do much good, with how many people are in and out of this place every day, but you might as well try," Ian said. "I'll photograph the scene."

While Ian and his deputy got to work, Janet called Debbie. It was earlier than she normally got up, but she would want to know what was going on.

"Hi. What's wrong?" Debbie sounded groggy.

"Someone broke into the café." Janet nearly choked on the words.

"What do you mean? Is everything okay?"

"They tried to get the register open but weren't able to. They broke the glass on the door and turned the tables and chairs over and spray-painted the walls."

"I'll be right there."

"Okay. Ian and Deputy Vaughn are here, but I figured you'd want to know right away."

"You figured right. I'll see you in a few."

Janet tried to stay out of the way as she waited for Debbie. She wandered over to the dining area and started to pick up a table, but Ian called out, "Don't touch that yet!"

She'd have to wait to clean up. "Can I at least start the coffee?"

"Let us finish up back here," Ian said from behind the counter. He was taking pictures of everything while Deputy Vaughn dusted a fine black powder all over the cash register. "We'll be done soon."

Janet stood in the dining room and looked up at the spot on the back wall where the crown had been spray-painted. What was that about? The picture that had hung there was one of her favorites. It was a black-and-white shot taken sometime in the early '40s, when the space that was now the café had been a canteen that provided hot meals and baked goods, especially doughnuts, to the service-men and women passing through on military transport trains. The picture showed three women standing behind a table set in the grassy area to the side of the depot. There was a briefcase on the table, an old-fashioned one with hard sides and a handle. It was a charming picture that depicted the best of the canteen, when it was a stop on the route of many travelers. Janet and Debbie had chosen it, along with the other historic photos that lined the walls, from the collection housed in the depot's museum.

Ian moved from behind the counter to join Janet and take several pictures of the crown.

"It's a weird thing to paint there, isn't it?" Janet asked. None of the other graffiti portrayed a picture, at least not one she could recognize.

Ian didn't say anything but continued to photograph it. Then he moved to the door, where Deputy Vaughn dabbed at a shard of glass that was still attached to the doorframe.

"Looks like blood," the deputy said quietly. He slid the sample into a sterile evidence bag.

"They must've gotten cut when they broke the glass," Ian said.

"That's my guess." Deputy Vaughn glanced up, saw that Janet was watching them, and muttered something to Ian.

In response, Ian said something under his breath, and the deputy nodded and responded. They didn't want her to overhear. Janet stepped closer.

"...like the auto parts store," she heard Deputy Vaughn say.

"And Smollen got out last week," Ian said in reply. "We may need to pay him a visit."

Just then, Debbie came rushing into the café. She wore a gray sweater over a pair of baggy jeans, her coat flaps flying behind her.

"Oh my," she said as she stopped short inside the door. "Oh, this is bad."

"It'll be all right," Janet said, hoping she sounded more optimistic than she felt. "It's not as bad as it could be."

Debbie had tears in her eyes as she looked from the tables to the graffiti to the glass on the ground. "Who did this?"

"We don't know yet," Ian said. "But we're going to find out."

A NOTE FROM the EDITORS

We hope you enjoyed Whistle Stop Café Mysteries series, published by Guideposts. For over seventy-five years, Guideposts, a nonprofit organization, has been driven by a vision of a world filled with hope. We aspire to be the voice of a trusted friend, a friend who makes you feel more hopeful and connected.

By making a purchase from Guideposts, you join our community in touching millions of lives, inspiring them to believe that all things are possible through faith, hope, and prayer. Your continued support allows us to provide uplifting resources to those in need. Whether through our communities, websites, apps, or publications, we inspire our audiences, bring them together, and comfort, uplift, entertain, and guide them. Visit us at guideposts.org to learn more.

We would love to hear from you. Write us at Guideposts, P.O. Box 5815, Harlan, Iowa 51593 or call us at (800) 932-2145. Did you love *I'll Be Seeing You*? Leave a review for this product on guideposts .org/shop. Your feedback helps others in our community find relevant products.

Find inspiration, find faith, find Guideposts.

Shop our best sellers and favorites at
guideposts.org/shop

Or scan the QR code to go directly
to our Shop

**While you are waiting for the next fascinating story
in the *Whistle Stop Café Mysteries*, check out
some other Guideposts mystery series!**

SAVANNAH SECRETS

Welcome to Savannah, Georgia, a picture-perfect Southern city known for its manicured parks, moss-covered oaks, and antebellum architecture. Walk down one of the cobblestone streets, and you'll come upon Magnolia Investigations. It is here where two friends have joined forces to unravel some of Savannah's deepest secrets. Tag along as clues are exposed, red herrings discarded, and thrilling surprises revealed. Find inspiration in the special bond between Meredith Bellefontaine and Julia Foley. Cheer the friends on as they listen to their hearts and rely on their faith to solve each new case that comes their way.

The Hidden Gate
A Fallen Petal
Double Trouble
Whispering Bells
Where Time Stood Still
The Weight of Years
Willful Transgressions

MYSTERIES *of* MARTHA'S VINEYARD

Priscilla Latham Grant has inherited a lighthouse! So with not much more than a strong will and a sore heart, the recent widow says goodbye to her lifelong Kansas home and heads to the quaint and historic island of Martha's Vineyard, Massachusetts. There, she comes face-to-face with adventures, which include her trusty canine friend, Jake, three delightful cousins she didn't know she had, and Gerald O'Bannon, a handsome Coast Guard captain—plus head-scratching mysteries that crop up with surprising regularity.

A Light in the Darkness
Like a Fish Out of Water
Adrift
Maiden of the Mist
Making Waves
Don't Rock the Boat
A Port in the Storm
Thicker Than Water
Swept Away
Bridge Over Troubled Waters
Smoke on the Water
Shifting Sands
Shark Bait
Seascape in Shadows

Storm Tide
Water Flows Uphill
Catch of the Day
Beyond the Sea
Wider Than an Ocean
Sheeps Passing in the Night
Sail Away Home
Waves of Doubt
Lifeline
Flotsam & Jetsam
Just Over the Horizon

MIRACLES & MYSTERIES
of MERCY HOSPITAL

Four talented women from very different walks of life witness the miracles happening around them at Mercy Hospital and soon become fast friends. Join Joy Atkins, Evelyn Perry, Anne Mabry, and Shirley Bashore as, together, they solve the puzzling mysteries that arise at this Charleston, South Carolina, historic hospital—rumored to be under the protection of a guardian angel. Come along as our quartet of faithful friends solve mysteries, stumble upon a few of the hospital's hidden and forgotten passageways, and discover historical treasures along the way! This fast-paced series is filled with inspiration, adventure, mystery, delightful humor, and loads of Southern charm!

Where Mercy Begins
Prescription for Mystery
Angels Watching Over Me
A Change of Art
Conscious Decisions
Surrounded by Mercy
Broken Bonds
Mercy's Healing
To Heal a Heart
A Cross to Bear

Merciful Secrecy
Sunken Hopes
Hair Today, Gone Tomorrow
Pain Relief
Redeemed by Mercy
A Genius Solution
A Hard Pill to Swallow
Ill at Ease
'Twas the Clue Before Christmas

Find more inspiring stories in these best-loved Guideposts fiction series!

Mysteries of Lancaster County

Follow the Classen sisters as they unravel clues and uncover hidden secrets in Mysteries of Lancaster County. As you get to know these women and their friends, you'll see how God brings each of them together for a fresh start in life.

Secrets of Wayfarers Inn

Retired schoolteachers find themselves owners of an old warehouse-turned-inn that is filled with hidden passages, buried secrets, and stunning surprises that will set them on a course to puzzling mysteries from the Underground Railroad.

Tearoom Mysteries Series

Mix one stately Victorian home, a charming lakeside town in Maine, and two adventurous cousins with a passion for tea and hospitality. Add a large scoop of intriguing mystery, and sprinkle generously with faith, family, and friends, and you have the recipe for *Tearoom Mysteries*.

Ordinary Women of the Bible

Richly imagined stories—based on facts from the Bible—have all the plot twists and suspense of a great mystery, while bringing you fascinating insights on what it was like to be a woman living in the ancient world.

**To learn more about these books,
visit Guideposts.org/Shop**